Marian Cox

The Poetry of John Keats

Philip Allan Updates
Market Place
Deddington
Oxfordshire
OX15 0SE
Tel: 01869 338652
Fax: 01869 337590
e-mail: sales@philipallan.co.uk
www.philipallan.co.uk

ISBN 0 86003 768 1

Printed by Raithby, Lawrence & Co Ltd, Leicester

Environmental information
The paper on which this title is printed is sourced from mills using wood from
managed, sustainable forests.

P00326

Contents

Introduction

Aims of the guide

The purpose of this Student Text Guide to the poetry of John Keats is to enable you to organise your thoughts and responses to the poems, to deepen your under-standing of key features and aspects, and finally to help you to address the particular requirements of examination questions in order to obtain the best possible grade. It will also prove useful to those studying the poetry in comparison with another Romantic poet. The guide contains a number of summaries, lists, analyses and references to help with the content and construction of essay assignments. The poems are grouped by genre, but where possible the guide follows the chronological writing order of the poems.

It is assumed that you have read and studied the poems already under the guidance of a teacher or lecturer. This is a revision guide, not an introduction, although some of its content serves the purpose of providing initial background. It can be read in its entirety in one sitting, or it can be dipped into and used as a reference guide to specific and separate aspects of the poetry.

The remainder of this Introduction section consists of exam board specifica-tions and Assessment Objectives, which summarise in detail the requirements of the various examination boards and their schemes of assessment; a revision scheme which gives a suggested programme for using the material in the guide; and extensive practical advice on writing essay answers.

The Text Guidance section consists of a series of subsections which examine key aspects of the poetry including contexts, themes and imagery, and notes on the poems. Emboldened terms within the Text Guidance section are glossed in 'literary terms and concepts' on pp. 84–90.

The final section, Questions and Answers, includes examples of essay questions of different types, and includes mark schemes, examination essay titles and a list of references.

Assessment Objectives

The Assessment Objectives (AOs) for A-level English Literature are common to all boards:

AO1	communicate clearly the knowledge, understanding and insight appropriate to literary study, using appropriate terminology and accurate and coherent written expression

AO2i	respond with knowledge and understanding to literary texts of different types and periods
AO2ii	respond with knowledge and understanding to literary texts of different types and periods, exploring and commenting on relationships and comparisons between literary texts
AO3	show detailed understanding of the ways in which writers' choices of form, structure and language shape meanings
AO4	articulate independent opinions and judgements, informed by different interpretations of literary texts by other readers
AO5i	show understanding of the contexts in which literary texts are written and understood
AO5ii	evaluate the significance of cultural, historical and other contextual influences on literary texts and study

A summary of each Assessment Objective is given below and would be worth memorising:

AO1	clarity of written communication
AO2	informed personal response in relation to time and genre (literary context)
AO3	the creative literary process (context of writing)
AO4	critical and interpretative response (context of reading)
AO5	evaluation of influences (cultural context)

It is essential that you pay close attention to the AOs, and their weighting, for the board for which you are entered. These are what the examiner will be looking for, and you must address them *directly* and *specifically*, in addition to proving general familiarity with and understanding of the text, and being able to present an argument clearly, relevantly and convincingly.

Remember that the examiners are seeking above all else evidence of an *informed personal response* to the text. A revision guide such as this can help you to understand the text and to form your own opinions, but it cannot replace your own ideas and responses as an individual reader.

Revision advice

For the examined units it is possible that either brief or more extensive revision will be necessary because the original study of the text took place some time

previously. It is therefore useful to know how to go about revising and which tried and tested methods are considered the most successful for literature exams at all levels, from GCSE to degree finals.

Below is a guide on how not to do it — think of reasons why not in each case. **Don't**:

- leave it until the last minute
- assume you remember the text well enough and don't need to revise at all
- spend hours designing a beautiful revision schedule
- revise more than one text at the same time
- think you don't need to revise because it is an open book exam
- decide in advance what you think the questions will be and revise only for those
- try to memorise particular essay plans
- reread texts randomly and aimlessly
- revise for longer than 2 hours in one sitting
- miss school lessons in order to work alone at home
- try to learn a whole ring-binder's worth of work
- rely on a study guide instead of the text

There are no short-cuts to effective exam revision; the only one way to know a text well, and to know your way around it in an exam, is to have done the necessary studying. If you use the following method, in six easy stages, for both open and closed book revision, you will not only revisit and reassess all your previous work on the text in a manageable way but will be able to distil, organise and retain your knowledge. Don't try to do it all in one go: take regular breaks for refreshment and a change of scene.

(1) Between a month and a fortnight before the exam, depending on your schedule (a simple list of stages with dates displayed in your room, not a work of art!), you will need to reread the text, this time taking stock of all the underlinings and marginal annotations as well. As you read, collect onto sheets of A4 the essential ideas and quotations as you come across them. The acts of selecting key material and recording it as notes are natural ways of stimulating thought and aiding memory.

(2) Reread the highlighted areas and marginal annotations in your critical extracts and background handouts, and add anything useful from them to your list of notes and quotations. Then reread your previous essays and the teacher's comments. As you look back through essays written earlier in the course, you should have the pleasant sensation of realising that you can now write much better on the text than you could then. You will also discover that much of your huge file of notes is redundant or repeated, and that you have changed your mind

about some beliefs, so that the distillation process is not too daunting. Selecting what is important is the way to crystallise your knowledge and understanding.

(3) During the run-up to the exam you need to do lots of practice essay plans to help you identify any gaps in your knowledge and give you practice in planning in 5–8 minutes. Past paper titles for you to plan are provided in this guide, some of which can be done as full timed essays — and marked strictly according to exam criteria — which will show whether length and timing are problematic for you. If you have not seen a copy of a real exam paper before you take your first module, ask to see a past paper so that you are familiar with the layout and rubric.

(4) About a week before the exam, reduce your two or three sides of A4 notes to a double-sided postcard of very small, dense writing. Collect a group of keywords by once again selecting and condensing, and use abbreviations for quotations (first and last word), and character and place names (initials). (For the comparison unit your postcard will need to refer to key points, themes and quotations in both texts relevant to the specific theme or genre topic.) The act of choosing and writing out the short quotations will help you to focus on the essential issues, and to recall them quickly in the exam. Make sure that your selection covers the main themes and includes examples of symbolism, style, comments on character, examples of irony, point of view or other significant aspects of the text. Previous class discussion and essay writing will have indicated which quotations are useful for almost any title; pick those which can serve more than one purpose, for instance those which reveal character and theme, and are also an example of language. In this way a minimum number of quotations can have maximum application.

(5) You now have in a compact, accessible form all the material for any possible essay title. There are only half a dozen themes relevant to a literary text so if you have covered these, you should not meet with any nasty surprises when you read the exam questions. You don't need to refer to your file of paperwork again, or even to the text. For the few days before the exam, you can read through your handy postcard whenever and wherever you get the opportunity. Each time you read it, which will only take a few minutes, you are reminding yourself of all the information you will be able to recall in the exam to adapt to the general title or to support an analysis of particular passages.

(6) A fresh, active mind works wonders, and information needs time to settle, so don't try to cram just before the exam. Relax the night before and get a good night's sleep. Then you will be able to enter the exam room with all the confidence of a well-prepared candidate.

Writing examination essays

Essay content

One of the key skills you are being asked to demonstrate at A-level is the ability to select and tailor your knowledge of the text and its background to the question set in the exam paper. In order to reach the highest levels, you need to avoid 'pre-packaged' essays which lack focus, relevance and coherence, and which simply contain everything you know about the text. Be ruthless in rejecting irrelevant material, after considering whether it can be made relevant by a change of emphasis. Aim to cover the whole question, not just part of it; your response needs to demonstrate breadth and depth, covering the full range of text elements: character, event, theme and language. Only half a dozen approaches are possible for any set text, though they may be phrased in a variety of ways, and they are likely to refer to the key themes of the text. Preparation of the text therefore involves extensive discussion and practice at manipulating these core themes so that there should be no surprises in the exam. An apparently new angle is more likely to be something familiar presented in an unfamiliar way and you should not panic or reject the choice of question because you think you know nothing about it.

Exam titles are open-ended in the sense that there is not an obvious right answer, and you would therefore be unwise to give a dismissive, extreme or entirely one-sided response. The question would not have been set if the answer were not debatable. An ability and willingness to see both sides is an Assessment Objective and shows independence of judgement as a reader. Don't be afraid to explore the issues and don't try to tie the text into one neat interpretation. If there is ambiguity, it is likely to be deliberate on the part of the author and must be discussed; literary texts are complex and often paradoxical, and it would be a misreading of them to suggest that there is only one possible interpretation. You are not expected, however, to argue equally strongly or extensively for both sides of an argument, since personal opinion is an important factor. It is advisable to deal with the alternative view at the beginning of your response, and then construct your own view as the main part of the essay. This makes it less likely that you will appear to cancel out your own line of argument.

Choosing the right question

The first skill you must show when presented with the exam paper is the ability to choose the better, for you, of the two questions on your text where there is a choice. This is not to say that you should always go for the same type of essay (whole-text or poem-based), and if the question is not one which you feel happy with for any reason, you should seriously consider the other, even if it is not the type you normally prefer. It is unlikely but possible that a question contains a

6

word you are not sure you know the meaning of, in which case it would be safer to choose the other one.

Don't be tempted to choose a question because of its similarity to one you have already done. Freshness and thinking on the spot usually produce a better product than attempted recall of a previous essay which may have received only a mediocre mark in the first place. The exam question is unlikely to have exactly the same focus and your response may seem 'off centre' as a result, as well as stale and perfunctory in expression. Essay questions fall into the following categories: close section analysis and relation to whole text; characterisation; setting and atmosphere; structure and effectiveness; genre; language and style; themes and issues. Remember, however, that themes are relevant to all essays and that analysis, not just description, is always required.

Once you have decided which exam question to attempt, follow the procedure below for whole-text and passage-based, open- and closed-book essays.

(1) Underline all the key words in the question and note how many parts the question has.

(2) Plan your answer, using aspects of the key words and parts of the question as sub-headings, in addition to themes. Aim for 10–12 ideas. Check that the Assessment Objectives are covered.

(3) Support your argument by selecting the best examples of characters, events, imagery and quotations to prove your points. Remove ideas for which you can find no evidence.

(4) Structure your answer by grouping and numbering your points in a logical progression. Identify the best general point to keep for the conclusion.

(5) Introduce your essay with a short paragraph setting the context and defining the key words in the question as broadly, but relevantly, as possible.

(6) Write the rest of the essay, following your structured plan but adding extra material if it occurs to you. Paragraph your writing and consider expression, especially sentence structure and vocabulary choices, as you write. Signal changes in the direction of your argument with paragraph openers such as 'Furthermore' and 'However'. Use plenty of short, integrated quotations and use the words of the text rather than your own where possible. Use technical terms appropriately, and write concisely and precisely, avoiding vagueness and ambiguity.

(7) Your conclusion should sound conclusive and make it clear that you have answered the question. It should be an overview of the question and the text, not a repetition or a summary of points already made.

(8) Cross out your plan with a neat, diagonal line.

(9) Check your essay for content, style, clarity and accuracy. With neat crossings-out, correct errors of fact, spelling, grammar and punctuation. Improve expression if possible, and remove any repetition and irrelevance. Add clarification and missing evidence, if necessary, using omission marks or asterisks. Even at this stage, good new material can be added.

There is no such thing as a perfect or model essay; flawed essays can gain full marks. There is always something more which could have been said, and examiners realise that students have limitations when writing under pressure in timed conditions. You are not penalised for what you didn't say in comparison to some idealised concept of the answer, but rewarded for the knowledge and understanding you have shown. It is not as difficult as you may think to do well, provided that you are familiar with the text and have sufficient essay-writing experience. If you follow the above process and **underline, plan, support, structure, write** and **check**, you can't go far wrong.

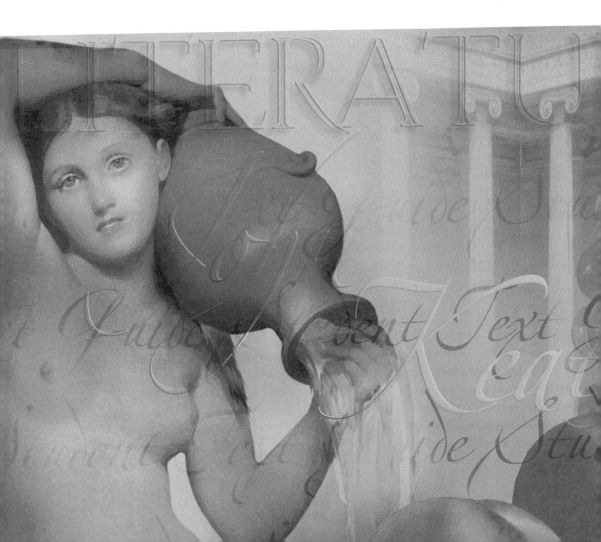

Text Guidance

Contexts

Assessment Objective 5 requires the candidate to 'evaluate the significance of cultural, historical and other contextual influences on literary texts'. There are a number of contexts in which Keats' poetry can be viewed.

Life and works

John Keats was born on 31 October 1795 in London. He came from an undistinguished family: his father, Thomas, was a stable-keeper from the West Country who married the daughter of the owner of a stables. Thomas died in a riding accident when John, his eldest son, was 8 years old. John's mother, Frances (Fanny), hastily and briefly remarried, and then disappeared for 4 years; John and his siblings were principally brought up by their maternal grandmother, Mrs Jennings, in Edmonton, Middlesex. Mr Jennings had left a considerable sum of money to his widow, and the family lived in some style. John was sent to the private school of Reverend John Clarke in Enfield, where he was taught the classics between 1803 and 1811. His mother, having returned home with consumption (tuberculosis), died in 1810, when he was 14, and left him an orphan. At the time and for some while afterwards, tuberculosis was regarded as a sign of decadence, being wrongly associated with venereal disease.

Keats' education at Enfield was followed by a 4-year apprenticeship as an apothecary-surgeon and the first year of Guy's Hospital medical course. He qualified as an apothecary in July 1816, but by then he had already abandoned medicine for a full-time career in poetry, having written his first poem in 1814. He was the only **Romantic** poet, besides Blake, who did not attend university. Encouraged by his friend Cowden Clarke, he came to know several leading writers of the time, which was an exceptionally rich period in English literature. He had already met Shelley by the time Leigh Hunt arranged for the publication of Keats' first poem in the *Examiner* in May 1816.

Keats' first volume of poetry, entitled simply *Poems*, was published in 1817. 'Endymion' (1818) was badly received by the critics, and he was labelled 'Cockney Keats' in a *Blackwood's Magazine* article because of his lowly suburban upbringing. In the summer of 1818 he went on a walking tour of the north of England, Ireland and Scotland with Charles Brown. His *annus mirabilis* (year of wonders), when all the great **odes** were written, was 1819; April and May in particular were remarkably creative periods. Keats was by now 23, and his happiness was threatened by his lack of income, which prevented marriage to his beloved neighbour Fanny Brawne, who was then 17.

His last poem, the **sonnet** 'Bright star!...', was written/revised in September 1820 on a ship bound for Italy. Keats died on 23 February 1821, 4 months after his twenty-fifth birthday; he was buried in the Protestant cemetery in Rome. He had a suitably **classical** tombstone depicting a broken lyre, **symbolic** of unfulfilled aspirations, and his own choice of **epitaph**: 'Here lies one whose name was writ in water.' However, he had earlier and more correctly predicted that after his death he would be 'among the English poets' (letter to Fanny, February 1820). It has been suggested that the last line of 'Endymion' Book IV should have been his epitaph: '[He] went/Home through the gloomy wood in wonderment.'

During his short career, Keats' poetry continually changed and developed, and he was entering on a new phase of literary exploration when he died. Having achieved his aim of creating the realm of 'Flora and old Pan', and to 'sleep in the grass/Feed upon apples red and strawberries' ('Sleep and Poetry' 1817, from *Poems*), he felt ready to move from the **pastoral** to the **tragic** mode; he wanted to make 'the agony and strife of human hearts' (ibid.) his next subject, and to write 'a few fine plays' (letter to John Taylor, 17 November 1819), having become less of a 'versifying pet-lamb' and 'more of a Philosopher'.

Keats arrived at the belief that human life is 'a vale of soul-making' (letter to George and Georgiana Keats, 21 April 1819) and that suffering is necessary to shape identity. What fuelled his endeavours was the creative tension between the suffering man and the rapturous artist, i.e. pain and joy. Keats' work is typified by this 'doubleness of angle' (Ricks, p. 146), and the 'complexity and open-endedness of his writings' (Stillinger, quoted in Wolfson, p. 246). For Keats life and love were not reconcilable; in each case the loveliness was counterbalanced by the transience. Poetry seemed tantalisingly to offer a way of resolving these conflicts, but in fact his message is inconsistent and contradictory, and only within a poem — and then not always without violence — is a serene conclusion possible.

However, Keats would not really have wanted resolution: if hot and cold were reconciled, they would become tepid, and therefore not a fully-lived experience to be the more appreciated by contrast with their opposite. And readers seem able to cope with, and even delight in, the **ambiguities** of the poetry:

> The key to understanding the universality of Keats's appeal is the fact that in every case the text may be seen to support the interpretation, even when the interpretation stands in direct conflict with another interpretation based on exactly the same text. (Stillinger, quoted in Wolfson, p. 257)

In Keats' work there is a friction between intensity, which he believed was what made art excellent, and a natural langorousness and propensity to dream which seduced him personally; he admits to having been 'addicted to passiveness'. He finally saw that the choice was between despair and energy, and he chose the latter.

Keats was a huge influence on later nineteenth-century poets and novelists, notably Browning and Dickens, who emulated his use of passion and sentiment, and on the early twentieth-century neo-Romantics, such as D. H. Lawrence, who shared his mystical reverence for all aspects of nature. The **pathos** of his **narratives**, his beautiful women, and his natural landscapes with their fruit and flowers also made him a favourite with the painters of the mid- to late-nineteenth century. The **pre-Raphaelites**, such as Holman Hunt, admired the pictorial qualities and strong use of colour in Keats' work and several of their paintings were inspired by particular narrative poems.

Keats is regarded as the quintessential Romantic poet, disappointed lover and doomed youth: he suffered emotionally and physically, he was dedicated to his art and to the ideal of beauty, and he died tragically young. Generations of readers have admired him for the quantity and quality of what he was able to produce in such a short life span, and under such difficult circumstances, and many of his poems are universally familiar and among the nation's favourites. In addition to the poetry, Keats' letters have attracted a devoted readership and are regarded as a literary work in their own right. They show intelligence, humour, and loyalty to family, friends and noble causes.

Chronology

1795   31 October, John Keats born in London, eldest son of Thomas Keats and Frances Jennings.

1803   Enters school of Reverend John Clarke in Enfield, Middlesex.

1804   Father dies in April; mother remarries in June.

1805   Goes to live with his grandmother in Edmonton, Middlesex.

1806   Mother leaves husband and disappears.

1810   Mother returns and dies of consumption.

1811   Keats is apprenticed to Dr Hammond, a surgeon, with whom he later quarrels.

1814   Writes first poem, 'On Peace'.

1815   Becomes surgeon's assistant at Guy's Hospital.

1816   Meets Leigh Hunt (who publishes his 'O Solitude!...' in the *Examiner*), Benjamin Haydon and John Reynolds. Qualifies as an apothecary but decides to abandon his medical career. Writes 'On first looking into Chapman's Homer'.

1817   Meets Shelley. First volume of poetry, *Poems*, published. Sees the Elgin Marbles; visits the Isle of Wight; writes 'Endymion'; meets Wordsworth for the first time.

1818   Visits Wordsworth; 'Endymion' published; writes 'Isabella'. Critical reviews begin to appear, and he is identified as a member of the derided 'Cockney School of Poetry'. He undertakes a walking tour of the Lake

District and the western Highlands of Scotland with Charles Brown. His brother George emigrates to America with his wife, Georgiana. Keats nurses his brother Tom, who dies of consumption. During the autumn he meets and falls in love with Brown's neighbour in Hampstead, Fanny Brawne (aged 16; Keats was 23); works on 'Hyperion'.

1819   The *annus mirabilis*: Keats writes many of his greatest poems, including 'The Eve of St Agnes', 'La Belle Dame sans Merci', 'Lamia', and the odes to Psyche, Indolence, Nightingale, Grecian Urn, Melancholy, and Autumn; also works on 'The Fall of Hyperion' and the play *King Otho*. He is engaged to Fanny Brawne, and becomes friends with the painter Joseph Severn, whose miniature portrait of Keats is exhibited at the Royal Academy; he visits the Isle of Wight and Winchester.

1820   Suffers severe haemorrhage; *Lamia, Isabella, The Eve of St Agnes and Other Poems* is published and receives favourable reviews. In September he sets sail for Italy, in the hope of improving his health; he finally arrives in Rome in November, where he stays in lodgings on the Piazza di Spagna (now known as the Keats–Shelley House); writes farewell letter to Charles Brown.

1821   Keats dies of tuberculosis on 23 February, attended by Severn, and is buried in the Protestant cemetery in Rome with the epitaph: 'Here lies one whose name was writ in water.'

Keats and women

Keats was thin, delicate and fine-featured, causing comment that he was effeminate in appearance as well as in his **style** of writing. In his famous portrait by Joseph Severn, painted in 1819, his pensive and feminine pose emanates sensitivity, and he admitted in a letter that he had a layer of skin missing. It is not surprising that he gave up on his medical training, given that the profession was a brutal one at that time. Keats' frail health was typical of that of young ladies of the period, who were notorious for being emotionally unstable and for playing the invalid. As the eldest of four orphaned siblings, Keats (aged 14) took on the roles of mother and nurse to the two youngest, Tom and Fanny.

By contrast with Wordsworth, whose belief in the '**egotistical sublime**' asserted the firmness and decisiveness of confident masculinity, Keats saw himself as a non-assertive 'camelion Poet' with '**negative capability**'. He chose to write in poetic **genres** considered less prestigious than those popularised by the robust Augustan writers (such as Swift, Johnson and Pope). These neoclassicists vaunted the manly principles of action and duty, intellectual enquiry, and restraint of passion. **Epic**, heroic tragedy, and satire were the diet of eighteenth-century male readers, and

sonnets and **romances** were looked down upon — even by those who occasionally dabbled in them, such as Wordsworth — whereas Keats found them attractive and suited to his temperament.

Keats' poems nearly all contain romantic love as a **theme** — whether spiritual or physical, between mortals or immortals — as well as other types of love: for beauty, nature and art. These preoccupations were then (and are still) considered 'girlish'. Although his contemporaries were also nature-worshippers, Shelley, Wordsworth and even Coleridge linked manifestations of nature with historical, religious, philosophical and political issues.

Apart from the actual characters in his poems, human or divine, Keats commonly **personified** objects or natural phenomena as female: the Grecian urn is a 'bride'; the sea has 'nymphs'; the serpent Lamia is female; Autumn is possibly female; the nightingale is a 'dryad' as well as a **metamorphosis** of the female Philomel; Melancholy is female; Mnemosyne/Moneta is the mother of nine female muses; Fancy is 'she' in the poem of that name. The voice of poetry in 'The Fall of Hyperion' is a goddess/mother/muse advising the human/son/poet. 'Ode on Indolence' describes Love, Ambition and Poesy as maidens and 'Morn' as female.

Keats preferred the aspects of the poet usually associated with female sensibility: pliability, changeability, the ability to melt into another identity, and to feel a full range of emotions. Keats saw the poet as necessarily passive and awaiting inspiration, like a flower waiting for a bee to visit. Anne Mellor (Wolfson, p. 218) shows how Keats **analogises** poetic creation with pregnancy, birth and nursing mothers, as well as with the related traditional female occupations of spinning, weaving and story-telling. He was interested in the female capacity for pity, sympathy and empathy, manifested by tears, passion, illness, madness and suicide (all attributed to women in the period and for a long time afterwards). The sexually active women in the poems are presented as predatory (La Belle Dame, Lamia), whereas the pure and passive women are victims (Isabella, Madeline). This perpetuates the customary view of women as belonging to one of two distinct categories, and which reveals his lack of experience with real rather than literary women.

Keats admits in a letter to Charles Brown (August 1820) that he treats women 'as roses and sweetmeats'. Women are portrayed as decorative and visually beautiful, but also associated with smell, touch and taste, the most intimate senses and normally those least dealt with in poetry. He often refers to flowers in the same context as women, or amalgamates them. Roses in particular recur, and are the flower which has represented women since medieval times (e.g. *The Romance of the Rose*) as a symbol of their sexuality. Keats saw women and roses as blushing, fragrant, soft, and waiting to be plucked; women and sweetmeats were delicious, tempting, and offered satisfaction of appetite. Freudians have commented on Keats' oral fixation, suggesting that he had not been properly weaned and wanted to compensate by putting everything into his mouth. There are numerous examples in all the odes and narrative poems of women being treated as edible or closely associated with food.

The question is whether Keats was a poet who was sympathetic to women and their concerns. The titles of his poems often contain female names or references: 'Lamia', 'Isabella', 'St Agnes', 'La Belle Dame sans Merci'. However, the female voices are, typically, suppressed. We don't really hear La Belle Dame's, Madeline's or Lamia's side of the story. Anne Mellor (Wolfson, p. 224) goes so far as to claim that Keats turns reader sympathy away from the female lover in all cases. This may be true for the Fanny of the letters too. He depicts women as inflicting pain on men as often as he depicts them as victims, and is only prepared to show unmitigated pity for those, like Isabella and Madeline, who are at the mercy of men. As with so much else, there seems to be an unreconciled tension in this case between Keats' admiration for female beauty and productivity, and his fear of the power it gives them. True to his 'camelion' nature, however, Keats is able to adopt the position of the viewer and the viewed, the seducer and the seduced — and therefore the male and the female — which gives the impression of some sympathy towards the latter. We see Madeline through the eyes and desire of Porphyro, but experience her dream and her sensations. In the odes the male poet tries to penetrate and fuse with the female psyche, to arrive at a blissful state of oneness; but he is unsuccessful according to some critics, because the distance between the two cannot be overcome, however hard Keats tries to make an imaginative leap across the gender gap.

Romanticism

The cultural period known as Romantic falls roughly between 1760 and 1848 (years of revolution throughout Europe and America). During this time writers gave a licence and a prominence to passion and the imagination in literature, particularly poetry. The first-wave Romantics were the precursor; Blake, followed by Wordsworth and Coleridge. Keats is one of the three major second-generation Romantic poets, the others being Shelley and Byron, who wrote in the first two decades of the nineteenth century and died young and in exile.

The Romantic movement — which occurred in art and music as well as in literature — gives precedence to the heart over the head, emotion over reason, instinct over knowledge; it deals with youth, tragedy, individuality and mystery, and its key themes are **ephemerality**, wandering, and rebellion. As put forth in Coleridge's *Biographia Literaria* (1817) and Wordsworth's preface to the *Lyrical Ballads* (1800), the imagination and the experience of the common man — and, for the first time, women and children — are of essential importance and deserve a voice. In contrast to the Dr Johnson school, which acknowledged only generality, the Romantics believed with Blake that 'To particularize is the Alone distinction of Merit'.

Since the Romantics were more concerned with the sensitivity of perceptions than with their formal expression, there is a tendency for their works to shift in form or **tone** within the same text, the mood of the moment being of paramount importance. A commitment to exploration and originality meant that they experimented with new forms of poetry, which sometimes rejected a formal structure or regular **rhyme** scheme, and a fragment or unfinished poem was a common feature of Romantic writing. Life and the affairs of the heart were considered too serious for humour, which is not much in evidence in the literature of the period.

Nature

Romanticism was inspired partly by the French philosopher Rousseau, who preached freedom and the need to return to the natural state of man, and by the German philosopher Hegel, who expounded a system unifying man and nature. Romanticism was a reaction to the Age of Reason, otherwise known as the **Enlightenment** or Augustan period, of the mid-eighteenth century, which expressed the values of the Industrial Revolution and public urban life. In contrast, Romanticism favoured untamed nature and private rural existence.

The settings for Romantic writing are therefore almost exclusively outdoors and in unspoilt countryside. Nature is a life force to be respected and revered; it has a symbol for every aspect of human feeling, and those who cut themselves off from or mistreat it will perish spiritually. Because the traditional poetic season was optimistic spring, the Romantics favoured melancholy autumn, finding it reflective of the inevitable loss, decay and grief of human experience, and the prelude to the inevitable end of life: winter. On the other hand — and if nothing else Romanticism is complex and contradictory — 'the romantic poet tries desperately to find some permanent and unchanging refuge in a world of flux' (Hough, p. 172). One refuge is the ideal of an early but beautiful death in order to escape the horrors of the natural process of pain and old age, and their attendant physical and emotional decline.

Inspiration

For the Romantics, poetry had to be inspired (that is to say unconscious and **organic**, not conscious and mechanistic) and an act of creation. They adopted the **Platonic** conceit of inspiration by a muse, who bestows a kind of divine ecstasy, similar to the enhanced state of the lunatic and the lover (see *A Midsummer Night's Dream* V.1.7–8), through the stimulus of the poet's imagination. However, the muse did not have to be supernatural, but could be anything visible or audible — such as a nightingale, a frost, the sea or even London at dawn — as long as it was majestic enough to inspire profound reflection and appreciation of beauty.

Since he was hailed as a pastoral poet and dramatist of the passions, Shakespeare was revered as a genius and his works were plundered for ideas by both generations of Romantics. Another historical source of inspiration for **imagery** and narrative was medievalism (represented also in the work of the pre-Raphaelite painters) in the form of legends and **ballads**, and their use of horror and heroism in the eternal battle between good and evil. For the second generation of poets, who travelled to Italy and Greece, classical landscapes and culture, including **mythology**, were also a frequent and important inspiration.

Fancy vs imagination

The seventeenth-century philosopher Hobbes saw imagination as **antithetical** to logical discourse and believed this made the poet inferior to the philosopher. Fancy was defined by Coleridge as more a matter of logic than creation, because it was under conscious control — a process of causality which subordinated constituent parts to form a coherent and proportioned whole from sensation, memory and thought. The Romantics rejected fancy in favour of imagination, which they embraced as an active plastic principle that shapes and embodies, making the mind of the poet analogous to the mind of God. To summarise their belief, fancy is a mirror, passively reflecting, whereas imagination is an illuminating power — a lamp. As Coleridge put it:

> The primary IMAGINATION I hold to be the living Power and prime Agent of all human Perception, and as a repetition in the finite mind of the eternal act of creation in the infinite I AM.   (*Biographia Literaria*, Chapter XIII)

The English Romantics believed that the imagination is in an essential correspondence with truth and reality. In a letter to Benjamin Bailey, Keats wrote that 'what the imagination seizes as Beauty must be truth' (22 November 1817), and he dismissed fancy as a hoodwinking, 'deceiving elf'. He quoted from a letter to his brother George, again when writing to Bailey, that 'a long Poem is a test of Invention which I take to be the Polar Star of Poetry, as Fancy is the Sails, and Imagination the Rudder' (8 October 1817). This makes it clear that fancy is only the means of propulsion and outward sign of movement, whereas the course is determined by the imagination, without which there could be no voyage. The Romantics went further than Shakespeare, for whom imagination was a respite from the cares of ordinary life and a tease to the thoughts, in claiming imagination to be a divine faculty offering a privileged perception to which ordinary intelligence is blind. **Metaphors, neologisms** and **pathetic fallacies** abound in Romantic poetry as flights of imagination superior to anything contrived or traditional, which included **similes**.

Mystery and magic

The Romantic philosophy propounds the view that not everything can or should be explained by logic or science, which destroys, for example, the awesomeness of the

rainbow. Coincidences and miracles are normal experiences for the observant, receptive and sensitive person capable of appreciating the symbolic workings of the natural order. Mystery and magic both feed and are products of the human imagination; supernatural events and characters therefore feature in Romantic poetry to represent the power of nature and the **fantastical** world of dreams. Fairy tales have plots and characters steeped in magic and mystery, and their plot devices were borrowed and developed by the Romantics: sudden appearances and disappearances, quests and journeys, metamorphoses and disguises, love at first sight, promises kept and broken, items lost and found. Secrecy and torture, grief and resistance were elements of chivalric romances which transferred happily to Romanticism, where they could be explored in more emotional detail than the romances allowed.

Gothic

In Romantic literature there is an overwhelming sense of ephemerality, of the transience and ravages of time, which steals youth, destroys innocence and betrays hopes. This concern coincides with the **Gothic** revival of the late eighteenth century, which was preoccupied with death, horror, medieval settings and dark atmospheres. Mary Shelley's *Frankenstein* is the most famous Gothic text of this period, but there were many others, and the Gothic influence is strong in such poems as Coleridge's 'The Rime of the Ancient Mariner' and Keats' 'The Eve of St Agnes'. The Gothic combinations of saints and demons, innocent maidens and scheming witches, youth and age, gave obvious scope for the staging of battles between good and evil, with the possibility of added complications or **ironic** twists. In addition, monsters and ghosts, as the literary descendants of snakes and dragons, could fittingly feature, linking medieval and biblical symbolism with that of classical mythology.

Religion

Beauty, passion and free will were the gods of Romanticism, and are exemplified by Milton's Satan in *Paradise Lost*. The arts played a prime role in the Romantic world view, since fine art, music and poetry are not only statements of independence capable of evoking the deepest emotion and providing inspiration to others, but they are also manifestations of genius and divinity. Enslavement to any orthodoxy was unacceptable, which left little room for conventional Christianity, and none of the Romantic poets subscribed to it. What is more, they developed their own brand of **pantheism**, a belief that every tree and river, hill and valley, was inhabited by a *genius loci* or local spirit. Nature, in all its moods and glory, was a substitute for religious worship and moral values.

There is no specifically Christian influence in any of Keats' work; his religion was the spirit of nature and artistic creation as manifestations of divine truth and beauty. His **epiphanic** moments of bliss came from the transcendent combination of nature and art.

Romantic heroes and heroines

Despite spanning many centuries, the youthful Romantic hero and heroine, derived from medieval court life (as in the Arthurian legends), have changed very little, even in outward appearance. Heroes have an exotic or aristocratic name and are tall, dark, handsome, sensitive, intelligent, witty, moody, athletic, rebellious, impetuous, seductive, strong, bold, charming, idealistic, independent. They are horsemen and swordsmen — or the equivalent — and lovers. Their job is to save their country, friends and helpless females, from themselves or their abusers, through brave and dangerous exploits. Heroines have foreign names (usually of three syllables and often ending in 'a'), are beautiful, long-dark-haired, unconventional, creative, emotional, proud, wilful, secretive, dependent, long-suffering and misunderstood. They provoke envy in other women, desire in men, and await deliverance by a knight in shining armour.

Unhappiness is more dramatic and evocative than happiness, so though they are beloved — unlike their sensible, restrained rivals — Romantic heroes and heroines are put to death or allowed to die, and thus fall into the tragic mode. Their passions, self-indulgence and impulsiveness lead them into fatal danger, yet readers are positioned to find them sympathetic because of their frustration with the mundane world of repressive conformity. They are destroyed by an inability to reconcile reality and imagination, as are Lamia and Lycius. The dividing line between Romantic hero and villain is a narrow one, hence the ambivalence inherent in many Romantic literary works: what they represent may be admirable, but their effect on others may not be, and society needs to protect itself from their threatening excesses.

Revolution and independence

Change and revolutionary spirit were in the air during the Romantic period. The Western world in the early nineteenth century had recently been in upheaval, with the American War of Independence, the French Revolution and the Industrial Revolution all within recent memory. Many feared or hoped that England would be next. It was typical of the Romantic poets to be supporters of liberty in any struggle against tradition and oppression: Byron died fighting for the Greek resistance against Turkish occupation, and Wordsworth went to France to support the revolutionary cause. The themes of revolution and resistance run through Keats' poetry, from family rebellion ('The Eve of St Agnes', 'Isabella') and social non-conformity ('Lamia'), to the large-scale overthrow of an established order (the Hyperion poems).

Wordsworth and Coleridge

From 1799–1807 Wordsworth lived with his sister Dorothy (and wife Mary from 1802) in Dove Cottage on Lake Windermere in the Cumbrian Lake District. This

made his environment rather different from that of Keats, the cockney poet who always lived in London. Coleridge's friendship with Wordsworth started in August 1795, as neighbours in Somerset, when they found themselves agreeing on poetic theory and both reacting against Augustan versifying. Coleridge was sound on theory, was an interesting critic, and had occasional flashes of genius, but he was not a consistent or disciplined poet and his subjection to substances, self-indulgence and women meant he probably did not achieve his potential. Wordsworth was less prone to despair; he had both standards and ideals, tempered by a political fervour which led him to France during the year of 1791–92, just after the revolution, where he met Annette Vallon and fathered a child by her. Having moderated his views in later life, he was **poet laureate** from 1843 until his death in 1850.

Keats and Wordsworth met at dinner at Ben Haydon's on 28 December 1817, as mentioned in Haydon's *Autobiography and Memoirs* (Hugo, p. 583):

> Wordsworth was in fine cue, and we had a glorious set-to — on Homer, Shakespeare, Milton and Virgil. ... And then he and Keats agreed that [Newton] had destroyed all the poetry of the rainbow by reducing it to the prismatic colours... It was indeed an immortal evening... It was a night worthy of the Elizabethan age.

Lyrical Ballads

Wordsworth and Coleridge published *Lyrical Ballads* together in 1798. Ballads were originally a genre within the medieval oral tradition, and therefore anonymous. They were sung by peripatetic minstrels to entertain the noble inhabitants of castles throughout Europe. They told of love, war and travel — the eternal and universal experiences. They were narratives of some length, and typically included dialogue and repetition. Wordsworth and the other Romantic poets were attracted to them because they represented everything which was antipathetic to Augustan Enlightenment. **Lyrical** means inbued with emotion; Wordsworth was able to add on to the ballad genre an examination of his own and his characters' feelings — which traditional ballads did not enquire into but stated superficially and **stereotypically** — and thus add personality and passion to a genre which already embraced magic and mystery. The *Lyrical Ballads* also show a departure from traditions in the genre, and indeed in poetry generally, by taking as their subject human beings normally excluded: children, women and ordinary countrymen, rather than legendary nobles and heroes, such as Robin Hood and Sir Patrick Spens.

There were three editions of *Lyrical Ballads* within 5 years: the first edition of 1798; the 1800 edition which included additional poems and Wordsworth's 'Preface' on poetic **diction**; and the 1802 edition which had an appendix to the 'Preface'. It is worth comparing key extracts from the Preface with the poetic theory expressed in Keats' letters and poems.

The 'Preface'

The 1798 edition of *Lyrical Ballads* was prefaced simply by an 'Advertisement' explaining that this was an experimental collection attempting to use 'the language of conversation in the middle and lower classes of society'. The importance of Wordsworth's 'Preface', added in 1800 and amended in 1802, is almost equal to that of the work itself, or indeed to any poetic work, in that it fundamentally redefined for the Romantics their aims and attitudes to the writing of poetry, and distinguished their approach from that of the previous generation of poets, whose highest ideal had been the emulation of the disciplines of classical epic or heroic verse. The amended 'Preface' of 1802 was the basis of the final version of 1850, the latter including a discussion of the question 'What is a Poet?'

The tenets of the 'Preface' were that poetry should use the diction really used by men, and should deal with the daily lives of ordinary people, which had previously been considered beneath the notice of poets or the interest of readers. Wordsworth coined the concept of the 'egotist or egotistical sublime', meaning that the individual and his or her thoughts, feelings and actions are axiomatically justifiable as the subject for poetry.

Similar and opposing views

Wordsworth made much greater use of the subject pronoun 'I' than Keats, which lends his poems an assertiveness and egocentricity open to accusations of pomposity and arrogance. Wordsworth's philosophy, though abstract, complex and grand, is more consistent and straightforward than that of Keats, whose ideas are somehow extraneous to his poetic effects, whereas Wordsworth's poems are more overt expressions of theory. Keats accepted the ideas set out in the 'Preface' only partially; he rejected Milton for Chatterton, but children and vagrants were no fit substitute for the gods and spirits in his works. He advocated the humble stance for a poet of chameleon-like **negative capability**, rather than standing on his dignity as egoist or superior being. On the other hand, Keats felt privileged and chosen as a poet, whereas Wordsworth claimed that the only difference between a poet and an ordinary man was one of status, not type.

Keats portrayal of women as exotic, alluring and beautiful, was very different from Wordsworth's Susan and Margaret and Lucy. He continued until his death to set his poems in medieval England, Renaissance Italy or classical Greece, which is a strong contrast to the Cumbrian and contemporary landscapes of Wordsworth. A glance at the names of their respective characters, including those used in poem titles, shows the gulf between the types of being they generally wrote about.

Another major area of difference between Keats and Wordsworth is in style: the former was not ashamed to use expressions of 'high poesie' in ornate diction and artificial **syntax**; the latter claimed that poetic language should be as prosaic as

possible. Though they may both have espoused Romanticism, there are more contrasts than similarities in their chosen modes of expressing it.

Coleridge's Gothic tale of the Ancient Mariner, imprisoned by a supernatural force and punished for an act of violence against nature until he shows repentance by acknowledging its sublime beauty, manifest even in the lowest of creatures, deals with themes dear to Keats' heart. Some critics therefore feel that Keats had more in common with Coleridge than with Wordsworth regarding ideology, content and style.

Where Keats and Wordsworth agreed was on the organic theory of creation. In a letter to John Taylor, Keats wrote that 'If poetry comes not as naturally as the leaves to a tree, it had better not come at all' (27 February 1818); this philosophy coincides with the views expressed by Wordsworth in the 'Preface' against a mechanistic tinkering with the creative process. They also shared a particularly awed view of nature and its bounty which amounted to an alternative **pantheistic** religion, less emphasised in the works of other Romantics. Another feature they have in common is the constant reference to the senses in their poems, though perhaps Keats uses the wider range. They both espoused the ultimate ideal of a fusion of man with nature in a state of oneness and perfect harmony.

Historical figures and references

Benjamin Bailey	(1791–1853) friend and correspondent
William Blake	(1757–1827) visionary early Romantic poet
Fanny Brawne	(1800–1865) Keats planned to marry her
Charles Brown	(1787–1842) close friend with whom Keats toured to the Lake District and Scotland in 1818; Keats' last letter was written to him
Robert Burton	(1577–1640) writer of the influential *Anatomy of Melancholy* (1621)
George Gordon, Lord Byron	(1788–1824) Romantic poet and rebel, who died in Greece during the Greek War of Independence
George Chapman	(1559–1634) translator of Homer; referred to in Keats' sonnet 'On first looking into Chapman's Homer'
Thomas Chatterton	(1752–1770) poet who died tragically young
Charles Cowden Clarke	(1787–1877) critic; an early friend of Keats who introduced him to many literary figures; Clarke's father ran the school in Enfield which Keats attended
'Cockney School'	name coined by John Gibson Lockhart in 1817 in *Blackwood's Magazine* to describe the new set of London writers, which included Hunt, Shelley, Hazlitt and Keats
Samuel Taylor Coleridge	(1776–1849) Romantic poet; coauthor with Wordsworth of *Lyrical Ballads*
Dante Alighieri	(1265–1321) Florentine author of the *Divine Comedy*

John Donne	(1572–1631) metaphysical poet, writer of love poems, secular and divine
John Dryden	(1631–1700) Restoration poet; 'Lamia' is written in Dryden-style **couplets**
Benjamin Haydon	(1786–1846) painter and friend; painted portraits of Keats
William Hazlitt	(1778–1830) influential critic
James Henry Leigh Hunt	(1784–1859) poet, essayist and publisher; founded and edited the *Examiner* in which he published several of Keats' poems
John Lemprière	(1765–1824) compiler of the celebrated *Classical Dictionary* (1788)
John Milton	(1608–1674) poet and Latinist; author of *Paradise Lost*
John Murray	(1778–1843) proprietor of the John Murray publishing house which published many of Keats' poems
John Hamilton Reynolds	(1794–1852) Keats' closest friend
Joseph Severn	(1793–1879) painter and friend, who was with Keats in Rome when he died; painted portrait of Keats
William Shakespeare	(1564–1616) poet and playwright renowned for sonnets and tragedies; major influence on Keats
Percy Bysshe Shelley	(1792–1822) Romantic poet and close contemporary, who also died young and was buried in Rome
Edmund Spenser	(1552–1599) Elizabethan poet; Keats admired and copied his imagery, **euphony** and rhyme
William Wordsworth	(1770–1850) 'The Lakes Poet', one of the best-known of the first generation of English Romantics; Keats met him in 1817; in later life Wordsworth became **poet laureate**

Literary influences

Homer

Keats' interest in classical literature and art had nothing to do with ancient history, civilisation or philosophy, but was based on a fascination with Greek legend and mythology, from which he borrowed many plot staples, e.g. metamorphosis. He was well versed in Homer, and a devotee of Chapman's translation of *The Iliad* and *The Odyssey*. The fact that the Ancient Greek poet was blind made him seem even more of a genius. The ode, a form Keats made great use of, was a classical verse genre.

Dante Alighieri

Dante's *La Vita Nuova* (1294) was well-known in Keats' time as one of the world's greatest romantic poems. Set in Florence, it is the poet's own account, in verse and

prose, of the tragic story of his unrequited love for the sublime Beatrice, who married another man and died at the age of 24. She became a symbol for romantic love and beauty, and marked the transition from courtly to romantic love.

Francesco Petrarch

Petrarch was a fourteenth-century Italian Renaissance poet who made famous a sonnet form (the **Petrarchan sonnet**) and the conventions for love poetry, i.e. the enchanting lady and the enthralled lover. His Laura, fictional or not, was the paradigm for an idealised, beloved female with religious **connotations**.

Giovanni Boccaccio

Boccaccio's *Decameron* (started in 1348) is a collection of 100 stories told by a group of Florentine nobles, who left the plague-ridden city in 1348 to take shelter in a palazzo in the Tuscan countryside. Many of these stories were adapted by later writers, including Chaucer; Keats found the story of Isabella here, as well as the earliest example of a **framing** device.

Geoffrey Chaucer

Chaucer, who wrote *The Canterbury Tales* in the late-fourteenth century, attracted Keats because of his Gothic and medieval atmospheres, his complex character portrayal, his management of verse narrative, and his sympathy for broken-hearted loves.

Edmund Spenser

Keats was attracted to Spenser's medievalism, epitomised in his verse epic *The Faerie Queene* (1590–96), which provided Keats with examples of romantic relationships, moral struggles, and pastoral settings used symbolically. Spenser, like Shakespeare, also wrote sonnets. Keats was particularly influenced by Spenser's 'gorgeousness of...imagery' (Wolfson, p. 189). Keats annotated his copy of *The Faerie Queene*. He was interested in Spenserean beauty, not his moral **allegory**.

William Shakespeare

Keats regarded Shakespeare as his main 'presider' (Wolfson, p. 192), and found him a source of insight into the suffering and contrariety of human experience. Keats' own annotations of Shakespeare texts focus entirely on suffering, and they are prolific, particularly in his copies of *King Lear, Measure for Measure* and *Hamlet*. We know that Keats read *Hamlet* 40 times; one of the reasons he could identify with the main character was his mother's remarriage only 2 months after the death of his father, but there are many other striking similarities between Hamlet's character and fate and Keats' own. Shakespeare had in abundance the **negative capability** admired by Keats, and was described by him as a chameleon who took 'as much delight in an Iago as an Imogen' (letter to Richard Woodhouse, 27 October 1818). Jack Stillinger noted that 'Keats has been likened to Shakespeare for some central stylistic similarities: richness of language, concreteness and particularity of descriptions, and an almost magical dexterity in harmonizing and varying the sounds and rhythms of his lines' (Wolfson, p. 251). A complete Shakespeare was one of the few books the dying Keats took to Italy as an inspiration and comfort.

John Donne

Donne was a poet of passion, secular and divine, and a fabricator of surprising imagery and comparisons. Keats' attraction to this early-seventeenth century metaphysical poet and his cosmological conceits shows in such sonnets as 'On the Sea' and 'Bright star!...', in which he makes the kind of analogy between the female body and a tract of land for which Donne is famous.

John Milton

Keats was impressed by Milton, author of *Paradise Lost*, as were other Romantic poets, because of his lofty seriousness and his confidence in assuming the mantle of poet and teacher (and because he suffered and went blind in the pursuit of his art). He was, however, a disastrous model for Keats, who was not a man of certainties and dogma, but a tentative and fluid thinker. Keats was forced to abandon his epic poem 'Hyperion' because of excessive Miltonic interference in the style and content.

William Wordsworth

Keats shared with Wordsworth a love of luxurious, complex language, a fascination with contrasts, and a belief in the power of poetry to convey the pathos of experience. He also shared the view expressed in the 'Preface' to the *Lyrical Ballads* that 'good poetry is the spontaneous overflow of powerful feelings'. His rejection of Wordsworth's poetic theory of the egotistical sublime helped Keats form his own theory of **negative capability**.

James Henry Leigh Hunt

Keats and Shelley belonged to a literary group associated with Leigh Hunt, which was dubbed the 'Cockney School' and was much derided by Tory literary critics such as Byron. Like Leigh Hunt, Keats was opposed to the antithetic regularity of the 'Rocking-Horse' rhythm of eighteenth century **heroic couplets**, and generally attacked the versifying of that era with energetic contempt. Hunt was Keats' first poetic role model.

The classical world

Italy (Rome) and Greece, as the origins of Western culture, were important to Keats and to the writers he read, and he made much use of their landscapes and art. The classical authors, mythological characters and references used in Keats' poems are explained below.

Adon[a]is	beautiful youth, beloved of Aphrodit and killed tragically young by a boar; Shelley dedicated his poem 'Adonais' (1821) to Keats after the latter's death
Andromeda	rescued by Perseus from being chained to a rock as prey for a monster
Apollo	the god of poetry, medicine and the sun; allegorically represents knowledge, order and enlightenment; plays a lyre; the intended hero of Keats' epic 'Hyperion' (cf. character Apollonius in 'Lamia')
Diana	goddess of the moon, fertility, nature and hunting
Dionysus	opposite of Apollo in Nietzsche's analysis of Greek gods and genius, and associated with **sensuality** and ecstasy (often induced by alcohol); also known as Bacchus
Elgin Marbles	marble sculptures from the Parthenon in Athens, consisting of fragments of the sculptor Phidias' frieze depicting warriors and some metopes; first displayed in the British Museum in early 1817 following their removal by Lord Elgin; Keats regularly visited these reliefs of gods and humans battling and cavorting together, and they were an abiding visual and thematic influence on his work
Endymion	handsome son of Zeus and the nymph Calyce; a shepherd on Mount Latmos, the moon-goddess Cynthia fell in love with him and granted him the gift of eternal youth
Flora	Roman goddess of flowers
Hecate	goddess of witchcraft
Hemlock	Socrates, the Athenian philosopher, was sentenced to die by drinking this poison
Hermes	messenger of the Olympian gods
Hippocrene	spring on Mount Helicon in Greece, thought to impart poetic inspiration
Homer	blind Greek poet thought to have written *The Iliad* and *The Odyssey*
Horace	(65 BC–8 BC) Roman poet famous for his odes
Hyperion	a Titan, identified with the sun
Jove	another name for Jupiter, the father of the gods in the Roman pantheon; equivalent to Zeus
Lamia	originally a woman punished by Hera, queen of the Olympian gods, and forced to eat her own children; Keats, following earlier writers, makes her a snake-woman
Lethe	one of the rivers of Hades; drinking its waters caused forgetfulness
Lilith	mythical first wife of Adam; similar to Lamia
Lycius	character in Philostratus' *Life of Apollonius* (second century AD), a source for Keats' 'Lamia'
Midas	Phrygian king who received the gift of turning everything he touched to gold
Mnemosyne	female Titan, responsible for memory
Muses	the nine female Muses presided over poetry, music and all the creative arts

Narcissus	beautiful young man who fell in love with his own reflection	Proserpina	Roman name for Persephone; queen of the underworld after her abduction by Pluto/Hades
Oceanus	one of the Titans; the god of the water encircling the world	Psyche	exceptionally beautiful woman, loved by Eros/Cupid
Olympians	the gods of Mount Olympus in Greece	Saturn	Roman god of agriculture
Ovid	(43 BC–17 AD) Roman poet; author of *Metamorphoses*	Thermopylae	celebrated battle of 480 BC in which a small force of Athenians and Spartans held off a huge invading Persian army
Pan	god of woods and pastures; he has the legs and feet of a goat, and induces panic in those who see him	Titans	original group of rulers of the Greek universe before they were dethroned by Zeus and the Olympian gods
Philomel	raped by her brother-in-law, King Tereus, she was turned into a nightingale		

Critical contexts

Contemporary

Keats was capable of self-criticism and arguably not as put out by critics as contemporary and later writers have claimed: he has been portrayed as the victimised artist torn apart by the Tory establishment. It was a popular legend in his own time that Keats was killed by the poison of vicious reviews, particularly those of 'Endymion' (1818). This view was perpetuated by Haydon's tribute in *Autobiography and Memoirs* (Hugo, p. 585):

> Keats too is gone! He died at Rome, the 23rd February, aged twenty-five. A genius more purely poetical never existed!... In fireside conversation he was weak and inconsistent, but he was in his glory in the fields. The humming of a bee, the sight of a flower, the glitter of the sun, seemed to make his nature tremble [...] The last time I ever saw him was at Hampstead lying in a white bed with a book, hectic and on his back, irritable at his weakness and wounded at the way he had been used. He seemed to be going out of life with a contempt for this world and no hopes for the other.

Shelley's preface to his 'Adonais' (1821), which was dedicated to Keats, continues this mythologisation:

> I consider the fragment of Hyperion as second to nothing that was ever produced by a writer of the same years. ... The savage criticism on his Endymion, which appeared in *The Quarterly Review*, produced the most violent effect on his

susceptible mind; the agitation thus originated ended in the rupture of a blood-vessel in his lungs; a rapid consumption ensued...

Leigh Hunt was also a fan of Keats and saw in him great hope for the future of English poetry. He wrote in the *Examiner*, December 1816:

> Many of our readers...have perhaps observed for themselves, that there has been a new school of poetry rising of late, which promises to extinguish the French one that has prevailed among us since the time of Charles the 2nd. It began with something excessive, like most revolutions, but this gradually wore away; and an evident aspiration after real nature and original fancy remained, which called to mind the finer times of the English Muse. In fact it is wrong to call it a new school, and still more so to represent it as one of innovation, its only object being to restore the same love of Nature, and of thinking instead of mere talking, which formerly rendered us real poets, and not merely versifying wits, and bead-rollers of couplets...The object of the present article is merely to notice three young writers, who appear to us to promise a considerable addition of strength to the new school. The last of [the] young aspirants whom we have met with, and who promises to help the new school to revise Nature and to put a spirit of youth in every thing,...is, we believe, the youngest of them all, and just of age. His name is JOHN KEATS. He has not yet published any thing except in a newspaper; but a set of his manuscripts was handed us the other day, and fairly surprised us with the truth of their ambition, and ardent grappling with Nature.

However, Byron's caustic comment that 'he was snuffed out by an article' (*Don Juan* XI.60) was not sympathetic: 'There is no bearing the drivelling idiotism of the Mankin' (Wolfson, p. 33) was one of his less offensive comments about Keats. Here is a more offensive one from a letter to John Murray in 1820:

> Such writing is a sort of mental masturbation — he is always frigging his Imagination. I don't mean he is indecent, but viciously soliciting his own ideas into a state, which is neither poetry nor any thing else but a Bedlam vision procured by raw pork and opium.

Even friends of Keats could be critical: William Hazlitt described Keats' style as 'all florid, all fine; that cloys by its sweetness', and J.A. Hessey opined '[Keats] is such a man of fits and starts he is not much to be depended on' (Bate, p. 86).

But no one was as indubitably harsh as the critics from the Tory establishment. In the *Quarterly Review* (April 1818), John Wilson Croker wrote:

> Reviewers have been sometimes accused of not reading the works which they affected to criticise. On the present occasion we shall anticipate the author's complaint, and honestly confess that we have not read ['Endymion'.] Not that we have been wanting in our duty — far from it — indeed, we have made efforts

almost as superhuman as the story itself appears to be, to get through it; but with the fullest stretch of our perseverance, we are forced to confess that we have not been able to struggle beyond the first of the four books of which this Poetic Romance consists. ...

It is not that Mr Keats (if that be his real name, for we almost doubt that any man in his sense would put his real name to such a rhapsody,) it is not, we say, that the author has not powers of language, rays of fancy, and gleams of genius — he has all these; but he is unhappily a disciple of the new school of what has been somewhere called Cockney poetry; which may be defined to consist of the most incongruous ideas in the most uncouth language...

[Mr Keats] is a copyist of Mr Hunt; but he is more unintelligible, almost as rugged, twice as diffuse, and ten times more tiresome and absurd than his prototype, who, though he impudently presumed to seat himself in the chair of criticism, and to measure his own poetry by his own standard, yet generally had a meaning. But Mr Keats had advanced no dogmas which he was bound to support by examples: his nonsense therefore is quite gratuitous; he writes it for its own sake, and being bitten by Mr Leigh Hunt's insane criticism, more than rivals the insanity of his poetry...

John Gibson Lockhart, in *Blackwood's Magazine* (August 1818), had this to say:

As for Mr Keats 'Endymion'... no man, whose mind has ever been imbued with the smallest knowledge or feeling of classical poetry or classical history, could have stooped to profane and vulgarise every association in the manner which has been adopted by this 'son of promise'...[We] must inform our readers that this romance is meant to be written in English heroic rhyme. To those who have read any of Hunt's poems, this hint might indeed be needless. Mr Keats has adopted the loose, nerveless versification, and Cockney rhyme of the poet of Rimini; but in fairness to that gentleman, we must add, that the defects of the system are tenfold more conspicuous in his disciple's work than in his own. Mr Hunt is a small poet, but he is a clever man. Mr Keats is a still smaller poet, and he is a boy of pretty abilities, which he has done everything in his power to spoil.

Victorian

Keats became popular in 1848 with the first publication of *Collected Works and Letters* (ed. Milne), which included 40 unpublished poems that had been left in the care of his friend Joseph Severn, who accompanied him to Italy and was with him when he died. The inevitable sentimental Victorian critical response was that, like Chatterton, Keats was a tragic youth whose glorious promise had been nipped in the bud. Robert Browning ended his poem 'Popularity' with the line 'What porridge had John Keats?'; the point he was making cannot be established

with any certainty, but he seems to be praising Keats' genius and asking what nourished it.

However, not all Victorians pitied or admired him; some found him irritating. The writer Thomas Carlyle said of him: 'Keats is a miserable creature, hungering after sweets which he can't get. Keats wanted a world of treacle!' (Matthews, p. 359).

Twentieth-century

The early-twentieth century perception of Keats was influenced by Freudian theories that he was deeply **sensuous** to the point of being orally fixated, but not a serious thinker. W. B. Yeats claimed that Keats died with 'His senses and his heart unsatisfied', and in 'Ego Dominus Tuus' (1919) wrote: 'I see a schoolboy when I think of him. With face and nose pressed to a sweet-shop window.' T. S. Eliot believed that 'Keats has no theory, and to have formed one was irrelevant to his interests, and alien to his mind' (Bate, p. 12). Freudian ideas about Keats are hinted at by William Empson's comment that 'Keats' longing for death and his mother has become a by-word among the learned' (Hough, p. 175), whereas Earl Wasserman coined the term 'pleasure thermometer' (Bate, p. 121) to explain how Keats intensifies warmth as an index of increasing gratification in the structure, plot and expression of his poems. He also talks about 'heaven's bourne' (ibid.) to explain Keats' search for the ultimate beauty, truth and pleasure. Graham Hough makes the backhanded compliment that 'Keats cannot refrain from chasing any descriptive butterfly that turns up' (p. 164).

Andrew Motion (current poet laureate) had this to say on Keats in a postcard biography:

> John Keats is the quintessential Romantic poet. He was the son of a livery-stable keeper, and dedicated himself to the pursuit of Beauty and Truth. In his 'march of progress and endeavour' he forged a style which was gorgeously sensuous yet braced with urgent social and political concerns, and lived a life which — in its shocking brevity and doomed tenderness — combined great good spirits with noble idealism.

Nowadays there are conflicting views: that Keats was a self-indulgent pretty poet who appeals to romantic women and effete men, but lacks robustness or modern relevance; that Keats had a social and political conscience; or, as Stillinger (Wolfson, p. 258) describes, that Keats is the epitome of the poet, and his poetry the definitive idea of poetry:

> Keats has been for readers since the middle of the nineteenth century a figure whose life, letters, and poems taken together are rich and varied enough to satisfy every idea of what a poet and poetry should be.

Language

Favourite words

The words which occur most often in Keats' poetry as a whole include 'feast', 'sweet', 'youth', 'rosy', 'cloy', 'luxuries', 'drowsy', 'fade', 'forlorn'. This diction suggests sensuality and temptation, the colours of the red spectrum, and a fascination with love; sex, passion and indulgence. It implies that pleasure can become excessive to the point of saturating the appetite, or inducing sleepiness. The words are mostly descriptive of transient states, and therefore the fear or expectation of loss and dulling of sensation is inherent.

There are many examples of particular references or events in the poems which support the claim that Keats' language and plots were influenced by his medical studies. Keats makes frequent use of flowers with medicinal properties, e.g. poppies; in particular he comments on the toxic or anaesthetic effects of plants. He refers to hot flushes, blood, sweat, tears, calories, saliva, pulses, fevers, brains, blushing, heart beats, and generally any condition involving heat, flame, intensity, evaporation and melting. Lamia's transformation is described by Sperry (quoted in Wolfson, p. 238) as 'the effects of a violent chemical reaction'. A more macabre indication of Keats' fascination with anatomy is the cleaned and tended severed head of Lorenzo in 'Isabella'.

Linguistic devices

Synaesthesia, clichés and transferred epithets

Synaesthesia occurs in different forms in a range of poems. For example, 'So cool a purple' ('Endymion') mixes touch with sight and also taste, since this phrase refers to red wine; it is surprising and oxymoronic, since purple is normally associated with fieriness (see Porphyro in 'The Eve of St Agnes'). The phrase 'purple palace of sweet sin' ('Lamia') is a compound of senses, as is Lamia's 'scarlet pain' and 'perfume light' ('The Eve of St Agnes', XXXI), and 'the touch of scent' ('Fall of Hyperion', I. 23–24). Sometimes the effect is of an overwhelmed and confused consciousness which cannot take in everything at once. (The use of synaesthesia to describe Bottom's dream in *A Midsummer Night's Dream* is an indication that he has had a mystical experience which cannot be translated into everyday terms.) Keats' practice of linking the other senses with the concrete one of touch prevents his imagery from seeming too abstract and makes the spriritual world seem more tangible.

A related technique to synaesthesia is the actualisation of **clichés**, so that outworn expressions such as 'fiery passion', ' a rosy view', 'faint with delight', 'life's a feast', 'her heart melted' or 'sweet dreams' take on new meaning through the combination of senses Keats evokes.

Another form synaesthesia takes is that of transferred **epithets**, in which the adjective would more usually belong elsewhere, as in 'placid sandals' and 'dreamy

urn' ('Ode on Indolence' lines 4 and 56). Another example of this usage is 'blushing shut of day' ('Lamia' II.107), in which the 'transferred' adjective prompts the reader to compare and contrast the literally blushing bride (and cliché) to the sunset, a closing which simultaneously ushers in an opening and the delights of the wedding night. 'Mid hush'd, cool-rooted flowers, fragrant-eyed' ('Ode to Psyche' line 13) and 'Touching with dazzled lips her starlight hand' ('Endymion' IV.419) are both examples of multi-sense combinations created by 'transferred' epithets.

Invented words

Keats was not averse to using **neologisms** and **portmanteau** words for particular sound effects, for originality, or to combine two or more ideas. In 'Endymion' (I.121) 'surgy' is a coining; Keats' use of 'gloam' in 'La Belle Dame sans Merci' (line 41) is also original: it has a lonely sound, conjures up 'groan' in **juxtaposition** with 'starved lips', and suggests 'loam' (i.e. the clay of the grave), as well as referring to a gloomy lack of light. In 'The Eve of St Agnes' (XXX) 'soother' is a portmanteau of 'smooth' and 'soothing'. This combination of meanings, with the 's' and long vowel, strongly evokes a rich and creamy taste sensation as a temptation and indulgence. In a letter Keats coined 'purplue', explaining 'I did not know whether to say purple or blue'. Coinages allowed him to get at least two meanings from one word.

Double letters and words

The language of Keats contains a high proportion of repetition, double letters, and repeated words or sounds. Keats was attracted to these forms of doubling because his aim was always to increase the complexity, richness and intensity of his diction. Excess can take an orthographic as well as an acoustic form, and pairs of letters or words have more visual impact than singles; look at how much of the diction in 'To Autumn' contains double or repeated consonants. It is revealing how Keats' misspelling in the letters usually consists of wrongly doubled consonants, such as 'nostrills', 'flaggon', 'boddice' and 'lillies'. In 'Ode to a Nightingale' (line 6), 'being too happy in thine happiness' has repetition of the same word and contains three sets of double letters (as well as a reference to excess); in 'Ode on a Grecian Urn' (third verse) there are six uses of 'happy'.

As manifestations of doubling of sound, Keats ubiquitously employed **alliteration, assonance** and **internal rhyme**. Words can also share implied meanings through alliterative or assonantal attraction, e.g. kiss and bliss, sweet and sleep, 'slippery blisses'.

Double meanings

The use of **puns, oxymorons** and **compounds** allowed Keats to conflate two ideas into one expression, or to introduce contradictions. Sometimes double meanings were useful coincidences for Keats; e.g. 'belle dame' sounds like bella donna, which means beautiful woman in Italian, but is also the Latin for deadly nightshade — an appropriate metaphor. The word 'mead' in the same poem is both an **archaism** for 'meadow' and a reference to a honey-based alcoholic beverage which links with the heavenly brew with which the lady intoxicated the knight. 'Darkling' in 'Ode to a Nightingale' (line 51) literally means 'in the dark' but also suggests a mental darkness or melancholy (literally 'black bile'), which introduces the idea of death in the next line. The use of the word 'mistress' in 'Ode on Melancholy' (line 18) can exploit the different suggestions of dominance, sexuality, superiority and medieval chivalry. 'Autumn's red-lipp'd fruitage' ('Fancy') is both red and makes the mouths of those who eat it red; the 'maturing sun' of 'To Autumn' is both growing older itself and making fruit ripen, just as the 'blushful Hippocrene' ('Ode to a Nightingale' line 16) is both blushing and causing blushing.

Sometimes a word conjures up another through similarity of spelling or pronunciation, so that a double effect is gained: e.g. 'plumed' contains the purple fruit; 'mellow' evokes 'yellow'; 'fragrant boddice' is suggestive of the body which has made it warm and sweet-smelling; 'lavender'd' sheets have a pale colour, a herbal smell, and a freshness by association with the French 'laver' (to launder).

Compounds (conjoined adjectives) are a noticeable feature of certain poems, e.g. 'To Autumn'; they add a stylistic richness to the portrayal of abundance to the point of saturation. Frequently the compounds begin with 'half-' to represent a mysterious borderline state which is actually more rather than less, since the **persona** has a foot in two opposing camps; half-asleep, for example, also means half awake, and as Keats said in a letter, one can enjoy the 'Luxury of twilight', which is neither day nor night, but both.

Oxymorons are **paradoxical** doublings, such as 'fine excess' (letter, 27 February 1818), 'perverse deliciousness' ('Endymion' IV.761), 'aching Pleasure' ('Ode on Melancholy' line 23), 'sweet enforcement' ('Ode to Psyche' line 2) 'pleasure's wreath' ('Ode on Idolence' line 18), and 'pleasant pain' ('Ode to Psyche' line 52), 'Happy gloom' and 'Dark paradise' (Endymion IV. 537–38), 'Pleasant smotherings' ('I stood tip-toe...' line 132). They reflect Keats' preoccupation with contradictions and his belief that sorrow is sweet and vice versa. He believes that pleasure is inseparable from or must be paid for with pain; it is 'Joy's grape' which lets Melancholy in ('Ode on Melancholy' line 28).

Catalogues

There is evidence of listing, the classical epic device, in Keats' poetry as a gesture of awe or admiration. The first **stanza** of 'To Autumn' is in effect a catalogue of nature's abundance, as is the description of the feast Porphyro prepares for Madeline in 'The Eve of St Agnes' (XXX–XXXI). The first stanza of 'Ode on Melancholy' is a negative list. Catalogues call attention to themselves as being extraordinary and exotic, suggestive of a heightened state of awareness in the persona or observer.

Long vowels

Long vowels are peculiarly frequent in Keats' poems, the most common and striking being the long 'ee' sound (perhaps because of assonantal attraction to his name), as in 'cease', 'cream', 'season', 'bees', 'breezes', 'Rhenish and the sleepy mead' ('The Eve of St Agnes'). Often 'sweet', 'sleep' and 'dream' occur in close proximity, as do clusters of autumnal words connected by the same sound: 'heap'd, 'reap'd' ('To Autumn'); 'glean'd', 'teeming' ('When I have fears...'). Long vowel sounds slow the **rhythm** of a poem and force a sensual lingering and quasi-**onomatopoeic** effect, e.g. 'oozings' ('To Autumn' line 22). They can also be soporific and create drugged, static, dreamy or otherworldly atmospheres.

Themes

The main themes of Keats' poetry are the interrelated ones of love, beauty and mutability, which are referred to and exemplified throughout the guide. However, there are several other dominant themes which recur constantly in various guises.

Embarrassment

Christopher Ricks' book *Keats and Embarrassment* (1974) is a central critical text for the understanding of Keats. Ricks claims that embarrassment is an important element in human perceptions and relationships and that the capacity for feeling embarrassed is an indicator of sensitivity and empathy, essential requirements for a poet. It is therefore intrinsic to a sense of decency, i.e. to an understanding of orderly and moral behaviour, and of the codes and conduct expected by society.

Blushing

Ricks shows how Keats was obsessed with the act of blushing, medically known as *ereutophobia*, which literally means 'a fear of reddening'. In 1897 blushing was studied in 120 cases, and the general symptoms listed:

> Tremors near the waist, weakness in the limbs, pressure, trembling, warmth, weight or beating in the chest, warm wave from feet upward, quivering of heart, stoppage and then rapid beating of heart, coldness all over followed by heat, dizziness, tingling of toes and fingers, numbness, something rising in throat, smarting of eyes, singing in ears, prickling sensations of face, and pressure inside head.
>
> (Havelock Ellis, quoted in Ricks, p. 7)

It will be noted that the symptoms are contradictory, heat and cold, the heart stopping and beating, tingling and numbness. Blushing is therefore an **oxymoronic** act both painful and joyful, innocent and guilty, private and public. In Keats' poems inanimate objects can also blush or flush; this **anthropomorphism** provides a sensual link between human and nature, whether personified or not.

In a letter to Reynolds of April 1818, Keats described hell as an 'eternity of blushing'. If one also accepts Ricks' theory that Keats' misspellings are Freudian slips, then 'rediculous' (letter, September 1819) is significant (Ricks, p. 59). Horace Smith said that Keats had a 'shy and embarrassed' manner (Ricks, p. 33); one of the reasons for this was self-consciousness about his height, or rather lack of it, which psychoanalysts interpret as a feeling of sexual inadequacy. Nature offered him the solace of forgetting about his 'stature' and gave him the opportunity to merge with something bigger and embracing.

Blushing is a physical response to a moral situation or vice versa, and as such would inevitably interest Keats. The blush of embarrassment rises with great frequency in nineteenth-century literature (in Elizabeth Gaskell's *North and South* for instance) and often in a quasi-sexual context or as a substitute for it. It is therefore related to shame as well as innocence, just as rouge is the pretence of a maidenly blush. Another paradox is that blushing is a sign of sickness as well as health, being indicative of fever and tuberculosis. By an imaginative transference triggered by self-consciousness, the innocent onlooker can seem as guilty as the wrongdoer by manifesting the same symptoms. Being seen blushing is therefore being caught red-handed, as it were, and one always tries to hide one's blushes as if one had been caught doing something private in public.

Since a visible state of embarrassment is caused by the same process as being sexually aroused, i.e. by the involuntary rushing of blood to a particular part of the body, they are seen as related by the medical profession. This connection apparently serves no physiological purpose, and so lends itself to having a moral one attributed to it. There are other factors about embarrassment which are relevant to Keats' poetry: embarrassment makes witnesses embarrassed, just as watching sexual activity arouses sexual desire in the onlooker; it is both subjective and objective, an inner feeling and an outward manifestation for others to register. Some readers find Keats himself embarrassing, because he seems to expose himself by being so emotional and so earnest, and does not mind how mawkish of sentiment or how flowery of expression he is.

Watching and voyeurism

Voyeurism is psychologically linked to pornography, masturbation, sexual fantasy, mirror-gazing and narcissism: they all involve a visual element of self-love, or a projection of it onto an unaware object; each is morally forbidden and a cause for blushing if witnessed. Interestingly, the phrase 'at first blush' means 'at first glance'. As Ricks (p. 87) puts it, 'the general sense of watching the naked is very strong in Keats'.

In mythology men and gods are punished viciously for being caught hiding to watch a scene of undressing, as in the case of Artemis and Actaeon. However, Keats saw it as the role of art to intrude on and encapsulate moments of intimacy and sublimity. The fusion of the viewer and the viewed can only occur if there is a

watcher. It adds to the sensuality of his poems that there is an observer who is being affected by the secretly witnessed scenes, and an observed who would almost certainly not wish to be seen when engaged in the private acts of sleeping, eating, blushing, praying and undressing.

Keats could only enjoy sexual congress vicariously, as far as we know, and had been brought up to feast on such delights as female nudity in classical literary texts and on marble sculptures and pottery. In the odes, Keats' persona spies unseen on the urn and on the amorous chase being enacted upon it; on the nightingale in the woods; on the personification of autumn drowsing; on the lovemaking of Psyche. In the narrative poems, Cynthia watches the sleeping Endymion, and Hermes and Porphyro separately take delight in watching women who imagine themselves invisible. In 'The Eve of St Agnes' particularly, but also elsewhere, the reader is given the viewpoint of, and therefore made complicit with, the hidden watcher and peeping Tom. We watch Keats watching Porphyro watching Madeline strip, and vicariously enjoy it, feeling embarrassed both for being there and for having caught them at it.

Consuming

Other acts we do not like being seen to do — because they give the non-participant viewer a physical or moral advantage — are eating and sleeping, but this happens a lot in Keats' poetry. The key diction Keats uses in connection with blushing can also relate to the consummating acts of sex and eating: melt, cloy, lips, breasts, panting, breathing, oozing, sweet, swell, burn. Like sex, eating is regarded as a private or furtive activity, or at least one shared only with intimates. It is an act of self-indulgence, literally and figuratively; but feasting is also associated with friendship, hospitality and enjoyment, an ambivalence which Keats seizes upon. Trilling says:

> [Keats] is possibly unique among poets in the extensiveness of his reference to eating and drinking and its pleasurable or distasteful sensations[... F]or Keats, the luxury of food is connected with, and in a sense gives place to, the luxury of sexuality.   (quoted in Ricks, p. 122–23)

In his letters too, Keats gives details about his taste sensations, describing in a letter to Charles Dilke (not sent) the eating of a nectarine as 'soft pulpy, slushy, oozy…like a large beatified Strawberry'. Keats' tastes, always for sweet stuffs, seem somewhat juvenile, and therefore embarrassing. In a letter he advises Reynolds to 'Gorge the honey of life' (September 1818). 'Gorge' is a very Keatsian word, meaning both 'throat', with connotations of redness, and 'incontinently stuffing oneself with rich food' — an experience shared by Keats' characters and readers.

Excess

Both whole poems and particular lines deal with the idea of extremes and excess, either physical or emotional. Keats' liking for superiority and extremes shows grammatically and conceptually in his frequent use of comparatives and superlatives. His own death wish and mood swings and those of his characters convey an unfamiliarity with or rejection of moderation. His poems — sonnets, odes and narratives — deal with the extreme emotions of joy and pain, often in quick succession, with no middle position. Excess is sought after and approved of because it is the only way to feel to the maximum and to live life to the full.

Keats often depicts overflowing, ripeness, abundance and luxury, all implying richness that cannot be contained and which therefore belongs on a different plane from the limited, mortal world. This is illustrated by lines from 'To Autumn' ('Thou watchest the last oozings hours by hours' line 22), 'Ode on Melancholy' ('And feed deep, deep upon her peerless eyes' line 20), 'La Belle Dame sans Merci' ('And nothing else saw all day long' line 22) and 'Ode to a Nightingale' ('But being too happy in thine happiness' line 6).

There is also something excessive about Lamia's infatuation for Lycius and the torture and tortuousness of her metamorphosis. All of the characters in 'The Eve of St Agnes', including the Beadsman and the drunken revellers, are extreme in their behaviour and attitudes — as are Apollonius, La Belle Dame and Isabella's brothers; they are all related to their uncompromising and pitiless counterparts in fairy tales and legends.

Farewells

There are various types of farewell evident in the poems, in which something or someone is forever 'Bidding adieu' ('Ode on Melancholy' line 23). On an obvious level, the poems tell stories of lovers who have to leave each other, usually when harsh reality intervenes (as in 'La Belle Dame sans Merci', 'Isabella', and 'Lamia') and dreamers who lose the subjects of their dreams, as in 'Endymion' and 'Ode to a Nightingale'. Humans have to say farewell to seasons, which is especially poignant in autumn. Even the Titans have to come to terms with the end of their reign in the two 'Hyperion' poems.

Keats also entertains ideas and objects only to dismiss them in the sonnets and the odes: 'Love and Fame to nothingness do sink' ('When I have fears…') and the urn is ultimately only an unsatisfactory 'cold pastoral'. The form of the poems, with the **strophe** of the sonnet structure and the 'return' at the end of the odes, often represents the rejection of an idea previously entertained. Keats says farewell to Brown and life in his final letter ('I always made an awkward bow') and his self-written epitaph renounces a belief in future fame.

Transience

The following feelings and experiences are depicted as transient on innumerable occasions across the full range of the poems: youth; beauty; health; love; life; virginity; happiness; dreams; pleasure.

In each case there is at first a sense of overwhelming delight, followed by one of painful loss. Memorable examples occur in the odes, where both the mood changes and the descriptions of process signify transience ('Where youth grows pale, and spectre-thin, and dies', 'Ode to a Nightingale' line 26). In the plots of the narrative poems, such as 'Lamia', love gets lost and joy is replaced by sorrow or death.

Immortality

The theme of immortality is apparent in Keats' envy of the gods and his identification with the role of the poet, particularly evident in 'Endymion' and the 'Hyperion' poems. The poet can soar to join the immortals, exchanging this realm of decay and pain for one of permanence and eternal beauty. He also describes this state in 'Bright star!...', 'Ode on a Grecian Urn', and through the 'immortal bird', the nightingale. Art, poetry and music have a timelessness which enables them to outlive their creator and their age. Fame is the nearest human approximation to immortality, ensuring that one's name is not 'writ in water'.

Dreams

Keats makes many of his characters dreamers, and gives them dreams which in most cases are wish-fulfilments and a contrast with painful reality. A dream is a creative act by the subconscious or divine mind, and is therefore like the writing of poetry. They are theologically endorsed in Genesis, in which Adam has a dream and woke to find it true (Keats quotes this in a letter). There are many other instances of dreams in the Bible, and visions in Shakespeare and in classical literature; Homer includes several in *The Iliad* and *The Odyssey*, among them the extended vision of a descent into the underworld for Odysseus, which also occurs in Virgil's *Aeneid*. In dreams secrets and solutions can be revealed, one can be reunited with the dead, and for a while what is lost seems not so.

For centuries dreams have been associated with lovers (see Mercutio's Queen Mab speech in *Romeo and Juliet*), to whom they deliver either solace or horror. Dreams provide scope for the introduction of the kinds of supernatural beings Keats was interested in: fairies, phantoms and gods. To Keats they were a meeting place in the imagination of the mortal and the timeless, not subject to the normal constraints of reality — a place where everything is exaggerated and 'richlier', to quote Wilfred Owen. An added attraction for Keats is that one can choose to daydream while awake, blurring the borderline between waking and sleeping. Dreams also create the paradox of the dreamer being physically immobile yet engaged in frantic activity in the dream.

There is a doubleness in being in two worlds simultaneously which can be contrasted for strong antithetical effect, as in 'La Belle Dame sans Merci'. None of Keats' characters are satisfied with the harsh real world they are doomed to inhabit — whether a medieval, classical or contemporary one — and so they use dreams as a temporary escape. Dreams or visions are referred to in 'Ode to Psyche', 'Ode to a Nightingale', 'Ode on Indolence', 'The Eve of St Agnes', 'La Belle Dame sans Merci', 'Isabella', 'Lamia' and 'Endymion'.

Metamorphosis

Keats often employs the idea of metamorphosis — between animal, human and god — which involves chemical and structural bodily changes that appealed to Keats as the medical student as much as to Keats the poet raised on Ovid's *Metamorphoses* and the classics. As well as being symbolic of immortality and the ability to escape from nature's laws, metamorphosis gives the potential for graphic description and dramatic contrast; Lamia's transformation from snake to woman is a celebrated example.

Subtler use of the concept is made in many other poems which contain sudden and extreme changes of mood, setting or physical appearance, but particularly 'La Belle Dame sans Merci', 'The Eve of St Agnes', the 'Hyperion' poems, 'Ode on Melancholy' and 'Ode to a Nightingale'.

Imagery

Keats was delighted by living and growing things, and meditation on natural beauty and the response this evoked in him were the central experiences of his life. Even his dreamscapes are realised through the observation of familiar aspects of nature and recognisable features of landscapes, though these are often medieval and classical rather than contemporary. He favoured natural images which can be associated with gain and loss, or which are binary opposites, like dark and pale. He wrote to Fanny (July 1819): 'I have two luxuries to brood over in my walks, your Loveliness and the hour of my death. O that I could have possession of them both in the same minute.' This reveals his need for the transitory and the opposing sensations of joy and sadness for sensual fulfilment.

Keats' imagery is strongly associated with the senses, and not just with the obvious ones of sight and sound, but unusually he gives prominence to that of taste, which he regarded as the most compelling and intimate of the senses. According to Haydon, Keats' desire to experience extremes of taste led him to 'once cover his tongue and throat as far as he could reach with cayenne pepper' in order to appreciate the 'delicious coldness of claret in all its glory' (journal, 1821). Taste sensations are usually accompanied by the appearance, smell and texture of the edible substance, so that often as many as four senses are called up simultaneously to create a full sensory experience.

The areas of imagery listed below are interrelated in a nexus of ideas pertaining to appetite and fantasy and are often used in conjunction with each other. They illustrate Keats' poetic themes, personal preoccupations and way of seeing the world.

Shades of red

Rosy is the colour particularly associated with blushing (see pp. 34–35), and the one most used by Keats. The blushing bride was traditionally transferred from her father's house to her husband's at dusk to conceal her embarrassment, i.e. her blushes at the sexual implication ('at blushing shut of day', 'Lamia' II.107). Throughout Keats' work evening, autumn and blushing are all associated — though traditionally dawn was the rosy time of day in classical literature. 'To Autumn' is full of blushing diction — 'bosom', 'fruit', 'apples', 'ripeness', 'swell', 'poppies', 'cyder', 'bloom', 'rosy', 'red-breast' — and a sense of pressure which correlates with the physical manifestation of desire and embarrassment. 'Fancy' (lines 13–14) has 'Autumn's red-lipp'd fruitage too,/Blushing through the mist and dew', and there is extensive use of such imagery in 'Hyperion' (III.13–22).

Keats' main colour scheme falls within the spectrum of red, from pink through scarlet to purple, and often includes the names of fruits or flowers, e.g. plum and rose. These colours occur either alone or contrasted with the words white/pale/faded, according to the hot and cold temperatures which themselves indicate the physical and mental state of the characters or personae. Red is the colour of wine, royalty and romance; it is also the badge of blood, passion and embarrassment. As Wasserman points out, Keats' poetry contains a 'pleasure thermometer' graded in degrees of warmth and redness (Bate, p. 121).

The phrase 'blushful Hippocrene' ('Ode to a Nightingale' line 16) establishes a connection between the classic colour of the wine, its effect on the human body, the hot-blooded deeds which intoxication causes, and the embarrassed blushes to follow. Dionysus/Bacchus was the god of wine and orgiastic revels, which further links the colour red with alcohol and sex, heighteners of heat and sensation. How appropriate Porphyro's name (meaning purple) is for someone to whom:

> Sudden a thought came like a full-blown rose,
> Flushing his brow, and in his pained heart
> Made purple riot. ('The Eve of St Agnes' lines 36–38)

Here blushing, desire and conception of an idea (a seductive plan) have been explicitly linked through the colour diction.

Heated heads

Keats uses brows and foreheads ubiquitously, e.g. 'burning forehead' in 'Ode on a Grecian Urn' (line 30). He marked lines in Shakespeare which connect the head and the womb, and which therefore talk of conception in both its senses — the lustful Iago in *Othello* does this. As Ricks puts it: 'Embarrassment, erotic feeling, and poetic creativity fertilize each other' in Keats' use of the 'hot forehead' (p. 163). The Keatsian syllogism would appear to be that if sex is red, and poetry is red, then poetry equates with sexual desire.

Flowers

Floral references are ubiquitous in the poems, since flowers are both life and death symbols, and are closely linked to ways of describing the stages of human life. Certain red flowers, particularly roses, predominate because of their traditional association with passion and romance; lilies are an obvious contrast to the rosy tint of flushed cheeks and brows and of healthy skin, and are associated with death and funerals.

Fruit

Again red fruit is favoured, such as strawberries and plums, as being symbolic of sweetness, juiciness, ripeness, paradise and the concept of forbidden fruit. Because they are usually 'globed', fruits are often associated with the female body, and the eating of fruit has traditionally been used as a literary metaphor for seduction. Red grapes conjure up not only red wine and its symbolism of intoxication and amorousness, but a picture of gods and emperors reclining and being fed with luxury food. The vine is an emblem which occurs and is referred to in classical and scriptural literature and art. Keats uses the word 'fruit' to mean poems (Wolfson, p. 95), since it is a biblical metaphor for issue or produce in a wider sense.

Dampness

Keats uses images other poets might think better of, like 'a mermaid in sea-weed' ('The Eve of St Agnes' line 231); its sensation of slime, slipperiness, fishiness, coldness, scaliness, and an unpleasant smell, rather cancels out the idea of mermaids as beautiful and amorous. Similarly, 'dewy' in 'Isabella' IX may be associated with dawn, flowers and sparkling newness, but it can also conjure up an image of wetness in the context — one of lip spittle and salacious saliva — which is far from seductive or attractive; the phrase 'lips, O slippery blisses' ('Endymion' II.758) may be clever wordplay but it is also unpleasantly slobbery.

Keats, perhaps influenced by his chemistry studies, was preoccupied with bodily fluids, but all dampness is potentially embarrassing and runs the risk of being disgusting. Ricks refers to Keats' 'disconcerting physicalities' (p. 102) and discusses his use of 'ooze/oozings' in 'To Autumn' (line 22), 'Endymion' (IV.667) and 'Isabella' (stanza LII). Like 'gummy' ('Endymion' I.229) and 'clammy' ('To Autumn' line 11), this is more likely to repel than attract; it is used in one of Keats' favourite Shakespeare plays, *Antony and Cleopatra*, in the context of the slimy Nile and its serpents. Ooze may be primordial mud, the essence of creation, both liquid and sluggish, in the process of becoming something else, clinging yet yielding, and all the other paradoxical qualities which fascinated Keats, but the primary reaction of the reader is usually one of distaste. Keats also refers to body parts not usually mentioned in poetry, such as 'pleasure's nipple' ('Endymion' II.868), 'an infant's gums' (II.451) or 'nostrils' (II.470), all

of which orifices and emissions convey a clinical view of the human body at odds with romance.

Sweetness

The word 'sweet' is used in 54 poems, and 81 times in 'Endymion' alone. It is a strong taste image and links with other sticky Keatsian vocabulary, such as 'cloy', 'honey' and 'ooze'. It evokes the thematic ideas of temptation, desire, melting and vanishing, like candyfloss, and the pleasures of sleeping and dreaming. Sweetness automatically suggests the senses of sight, touch, taste and smell, and can also be applied to sound. One can have too much of sweetness, 'like a wasp drowning in jam' (letter), and some readers feel that way about Keats' poetry, which has been described as 'nauseous sweetness' (Alexander Smith, quoted in Matthews, p. 365).

Eating

Eating, or the desire/intention to eat, occurs regularly in Keats' poetry and represents a hunger for passion, beauty, pleasure and life. Keats was attracted to this activity because it combines the sensations of warmth, indulgence, romance, and satisfaction of appetite, at least temporarily — hence the peculiar insistence on the sense of taste in Keats' poetry. Eating and drinking are regular activities in the poems, described in lingering detail. Food and drink do not always actually pass the lips; sometimes characters or the persona fantasise about it, or describe others indulging in it, or use it to provide imagery. There are references to consuming in 'Ode on Melancholy', 'To Autumn', 'The Eve of St Agnes', 'Lamia' and 'Isabella'.

Feasting as a concept is symbolic of other desires, and there is a long literary and religious tradition of this. The preparation of special meals has always been a way of demonstrating love, and the refusal to eat it a way of rejecting it. Lovers who can't get enough of their loved ones wish to consume them to prevent others from looking at them, or to savour the prized flesh. Many terms of endearment or sexual desire are food-related (e.g. tart, crumpet, honey, dishy, tasty); sex and eating have been associated since Eve offered Adam an apple, whereas fasting by the pious signifies abstinence from the sins of the flesh. Women have traditionally been wooed with chocolates and other sweets; male writers have always described the female beloved as a collection of edible parts: lips like cherries, skin like milk etc.

Mouths

Mouths are mentioned whole and as constituent parts: lips, palates, saliva, tongues and throats. They are all erogenous as well as taste zones. Even bees have lips ('Ode on Melancholy' line 24) and Autumn has 'red-lipped fruitage' ('Fancy'). Many characters do things with their mouths in the poems: talking, singing, praying, kissing, drinking, sipping, sucking. It is an erotic act to put food into the mouth of a loved one. Gods and poets speak to their audience; from their mouths truths and wisdom are uttered.

Breasts

Breasts, nipples, and milk enter into the equation with mouths to reinforce the general theme of hunger, thirst and appetite. Keats uses a surprising number of round and spherical shapes — such as caves, grapes, apples, eyes, bubbles, buds, tears and lakes. This has led to the psychoanalytical reading that he is orally fixated; in a letter to Fanny in September 1819 he admitted: 'I have been endeavouring to wean myself from you.' As Ricks puts it: 'No one would deny that Keats was preoccupied with breasts and that sometimes he could not think in their vicinity.' Sometimes he substituted cheeks, peaches, and pillows (all in soft, plump, fragrant pairs), as in 'Bright star!…', thus linking blushing, sleeping, eating and beds. It has been suggested that Keats Oedipally conflated Fanny with his mother (whom Keats refers to only once in the whole of his letters). They shared a name and the role of an absent comfort and unattainable desire.

Drowsiness

There are many references to sleepiness or actual sleeping in the poems, often as a preamble or postscript to a dream sequence. Keats uses a semantic cluster of words built around this idea: opium, poppies, fumes, mist, draught, elixir. Opium, in the form of liquid laudanum, was a common addiction among Keats' contemporaries, and is associated with poets' creative visions. Drowsiness is a half-and-half state, a fading away, and a loss of the senses, all of which interested Keats.

Bees

Bees make honey, and so are producers of sweetness, like poets. Bees also provide an **onomatopoeic** murmuring to create the effect of relaxed drowsiness. They feature large in classical **pastoral** literature and are particularly associated with the earthly paradise of Arcadia in ancient Greece. They are a useful image for Keats in being a synthesis of flowers and food, thereby combining the senses of sight, smell and taste with a sound effect. Like the gods, they sip nectar, the divine equivalent to humans drinking wine.

Warmth

Associated with youth and passion, the rising of the external or body temperature is an image of the glow of physical desire, intimacy and indulgence. It can be used as a warning contrast to those feeling pale or cold, like the loitering knight, the Beadsman and Apollonius, who are excluded from dream fantasies and from warm beds and breasts. Keats often condemns the real world for lacking warmth.

Bubbles

Bubbles (mentioned in several poems and a common word in Shakespeare) are objects of airy beauty which melt and vanish, and therefore symbolise ephemerality. A combination of liquid and air, they are in constant motion and have a transparency and vulnerability which fascinate the watcher, as if they have been produced by magic.

Notes on the poems

The sonnets

Keats experimented throughout his writing career with sonnets, the traditional form of Elizabethan poetry which was still popular with Romantic poets and was adopted by female poets in the nineteenth century. The combination of elegance and sensibility meant that the sonnet was prized as the epitome of artistic expression by lyrical poets. Originally sonnets concerned unrequited love, worship of divinity, and the transience of earthly joys, all topics which appealed to Keats. Their formal constraint demanded a compactness of syntax and a richness of diction which often led to obscurity and ambiguity.

All true sonnets consist of 14 lines of **iambic pentameter** and have a rhyme scheme, but there are two distinct main types. The first, imported to England with the Renaissance, was the Italian or Petrarchan sonnet: an **octave/octet** followed by a **sestet** with a turn or strophe at the transition point. 'Written on the day Mr Leigh Hunt left Prison' and 'To Leigh Hunt, Esq.' are both examples of Petrarchan sonnets. Later, in the sixteenth century, the English or **Shakespearean sonnet** was born: three **quatrains** followed by a final pair of lines which form the turn or crux. 'When I have fears...' is an example of a Shakespearean sonnet. The Petrarchan rhyme scheme is abba, abba, cdcdcd/cdecde; the Shakespearean is abab, cdcd, efef, gg. Keats mainly wrote Petrarchan sonnets to start with, but after 1818 he adopted the Shakespearean, probably because it was less restrictive.

Many of the sonnets can be usefully paired to bring out similarities of beliefs, values and concerns. Students need to study closely those included in their set selection, and be able to summarise the content, paraphrase the views expressed, and comment on particularly significant words and phrases. The background to the most well-known of Keats' sonnets is given below.

'Written on the day that Mr Leigh Hunt left Prison' and 'To Leigh Hunt, Esq.'

Leigh Hunt was Keats' early mentor and publisher of his poems in the *Examiner*. He was a radical and attracted attacks from Tory critics and writers. He was imprisoned for libel after attacking the government in 1812.

'On first looking into Chapman's Homer' and 'On first seeing the Elgin Marbles'

In October 1816 Keats was lent Chapman's English translation of Homer's *The Iliad* and *The Odyssey* for the first time. He had previously used Pope's translation. He read it one evening with his friend Cowden Clarke and was so enthralled that he wrote this sonnet during the night. The Elgin Marbles were on display in the British Museum and Keats saw them there in early 1817.

'Keen, fitful gusts are whisp'ring...' and 'Addressed to the same 'Great spirits'

The first was written in September 1816 as a tribute to Leigh Hunt, from whose cottage Keats is walking homeward on a chilly autumn night and with whom he has just been reading Milton's 'Lycidas'. He refers to Milton's drowned friend Edward King and to Petrarch's beloved Laura.

The second was written 2 months later and addressed to Benjamin Haydon. It praises Wordsworth (who lived near Helvellyn) and Hunt ('he of the rose' because he had rose-coloured wallpaper) as fellow great spirits.

'On the Sea' and 'When I have fears...'

The first was written in April 1817 on the Isle of Wight. It was included in a letter to Reynolds. Keats first saw the sea in the summer of 1816.

The second was written in January 1818, and is Keats' first sonnet in Shakespearean form. It refers to a chance meeting with an unknown lady in Vauxhall Gardens some years before. At this time Keats had no apparent reason to believe that he would soon literally 'cease to be', but during this month his brother Tom started spitting blood, which is a sure sign of the highly infectious disease tuberculosis.

'On sitting down to read *King Lear* once again' and 'On visiting the tomb of Burns'

In January 1818 Keats was rereading *King Lear* because he was planning 'Hyperion' and the former was his model for a stern epic of fall from power. It is Shakespeare's most mature and sublime tragedy (1605) and concerns the painful overthrow of an ancient king of an ancient England.

Robert Burns was the most famous Scottish poet, who died in 1796. Keats visited his tomb in Dumfries during his walking tour of Scotland with Charles Brown in the summer of 1818, when the second sonnet was written.

'If by dull rhymes our English must be chain'd'

Written in April or May 1819, this sonnet refers to the convention that English poetry should be modelled on classical rhyme schemes, with which Keats disagreed. Andromeda and Midas are mythological characters.

'To Mrs Reynolds's Cat'

Written in January 1818, this is a parody of a Milton sonnet. Keats was spending a great deal of time with his friend Reynolds during this period. Poems about cats had been popularised by Thomas Gray's 'Ode on the Death of a Favourite Cat, Drowned in a Tub of Gold Fishes' (1748).

'Bright star!...'

First written at an uncertain date prior to April 1819, this was originally thought to be the last poem written by Keats owing to an error by Joseph Severn, who saw Keats reworking it on the ship to Italy in the autumn of 1820. It was written on a blank page in a copy of Shakespeare's poems, facing 'A Lover's Complaint', and is assumed to refer to Keats' love for Fanny Brawne.

The odes

'Ode to Psyche'

This is considered the most cheerful, and perhaps the most bland, of Keats' odes, and is certainly one of the least popular, perhaps because it is very stylised. It is addressed to the female classical deity of that name, and has as its theme the renewal of poetry; Psyche is a victim of the historical process and Keats offers to become her modern priest. Her name allegorically means soul, and Keats described life as a 'vale of Soul-making' (letter to George and Georgiana Keats, February 1819) just before composing the ode in April. In the ode Keats expresses his respect for the main tenet of Romanticism, that man's individual powers of creation are worthy of exploration and veneration. The poem has a sense of historical perspective not present in the other odes, except tangentially in 'Ode to a Nightingale'.

Mythological source

Keats found the background for this ode in a Roman satirical work called *The Golden Ass* by Apuleius. According to the myth, Venus grows jealous when men desert her shrines to pay homage to a mortal girl, Psyche, instead. To punish Psyche, Venus commands her son Cupid to make Psyche fall in love with the most loathsome creature alive (compare Titania's punishment in *A Midsummer Night's Dream*). However, Cupid himself falls in love with her and visits her in a miraculous palace at night, on condition that she must never see him or she will lose him. One night, she lights a lamp to discover who her lover is, and, angry at being disobeyed, Cupid abandons her. Desolate, Psyche wanders the earth looking for him in vain, until Cupid finally takes pity on her and asks Jove to grant her immortality so that he can acknowledge her as his wife.

There are many aspects of the myth which would have appealed to Keats: falling in love; a relationship between a human and a god; the worship of a female;

punishment and suffering; loss and grief; secrecy and night-time; becoming immortal; the hidden watcher.

Language and style

The ode contains many examples of poetic devices and language in the **grand style**:

- **apostrophe** (lines 1 and 36)
- **chiasmus** — 'sweet enforcement and remembrance dear' (line 2)
- **oxymoron** — 'sweet enforcement' (line 2); 'delicious moan' (line 30); 'pleasant pain' (line 52)
- **synecdoche** — fans are a metaphor for wings, representing divinity (line 41)
- **archaic diction** — 'fane' for temple (line 50)
- **superlatives** — lines 10, 24, 36
- **repetition** — lines 22, 37, 54, 55
- **rhetorical** questions — lines 6, 22
- **exclamations** — lines 23, 25, 67

The phrase 'soft-conched ear' (line 4) is typically Keatsian. Compound adjectives such as this enable Keats to create a richness and density of sounds and meanings, doubling the effect of the imagery. There are many used throughout the poem. Since 'conch' means shell, its juxtaposition with 'soft' is an oxymoron. It is also typical of Keats to describe body parts and natural objects as being interchangeable through **anthropomorphism** — see 'fragrant-eyed' (line 13) flowers. Multiple senses are evoked by this and other compounds, such as 'cool-rooted' (line 13), 'silver-white' (line 14), 'pale-mouth'd' (line 35), 'moss-lain' (line 57).

The third stanza contains many lines beginning with a negative. This rhetorical use of **anaphora** conveys a double injustice and loss by stressing not only what Psyche does not have, but also what others do have. The stylistic device creates a liturgical list — a series of images moving through aspects of a church service — to support his argument, show reverence, and build up tension. It is similar to the opening of 'Ode on Melancholy' and compels attention.

Images and themes

The poem contains many references to aspects of the classical Greek landscape and gives a general impression of an unspoilt, tranquil, Arcadian paradise. Its natural features are rugged steep mountains, temples, clusters of trees, moss, streams, breezes, birds, bees, nymphs, gods. This inspirational setting also occurs in 'Lamia', the two 'Hyperion' poems, 'Ode on a Grecian Urn', 'Ode on Melancholy' and 'Endymion'.

Love and poetry are the causes of celebration in the ode, and the imagery of light is the main vehicle for conveying the euphoria. Phoebe and Vesper (goddesses of moon and evening star respectively) do not shed much light compared to the 'lucent' Psyche. The final image is of a window glowing and beckoning the traveller

in the night. It is through light that the eye perceives beauty, and it is the lamp of imagination which has created the vision of love.

The poem celebrates the power of the creative artist to bring something to life in the 'untrodden region of [the] mind', meaning the imagination or soul, the province of Psyche. There is a sexual implication in the final image of the window being open to let warm love in, and a celebration of the union of both male and female, and of heaven and earth. Other joyous factors are:

- the rich and romantic colours of purple ('Tyrian') and pink ('aurorean')
- the freedom of movement
- the freshness and abundance of spring and youth
- the purity of true love (the dove is white and believed to mate for life)

As is fitting in a hymn, the middle of the poem consists of **eulogistic** exclamations with no main verb. As befits a prayer, there is a promise to the deity of future exemplary behaviour, after a placatory address expressing repentance and a desire for forgiveness for man's insensitivity and neglect. Confession is followed by a sense of release and peace, and a desire to celebrate with music and incense.

'Ode on Indolence'

This is the least well-known of the odes, written in late-spring 1819. Keats suffered from spells of idleness, and understood the seductive attraction of indolence, a drowsy numbness of the body and mind. The gods and ancients were much given, according to art and literature, to reclining indolently, either draping themselves around cool marble or napping in bowery glades, a temptation in hot climates. Indolence is associated with self-indulgence, feasting, dallying and being entertained by music, and is therefore linked to our perception of the medieval lifestyle as well as the classical one (Shakespeare also creates such an atmosphere in Orsino's palace for the opening of *Twelfth Night*). The fellow state of indolence is melancholy, since one has opportunity for morbid reflection on human transience. Christianity condemns sloth (one of the seven deadly sins) and the Bible exhorts man to produce and multiply and work for a living, so indolence is often accompanied by guilt.

Biblical allusions

The **epigraph** of the poem is 'They toil not neither do they spin', which alludes to Matthew 4.28: 'Consider the lilies of the field, how they grow; they toil not, neither do they spin.' As a result of the Fall of Man, caused by the eating of the forbidden fruit of the Tree of Knowledge, the human race was sentenced to a lifetime of toil: digging for men and spinning for women. This is relevant to the poem because Keats envied the immortals their gift of leisure, denied to man. Lilies (a favourite literary flower for Keats) are used in the biblical quotation as an example of how God provides and therefore man need not work, an alternative and more attractive message.

This ode is similar in content and feeling to Milton's 'Il Penseroso', where the concept of activity is banished as 'vain deluding Joy'. In the ode, the persona (presumably Keats) is enjoying an indolent May afternoon when three temptations, or urges to activity, appear before him — Love, Ambition and Poetry — generated by his guilt. He is initially tempted to follow them and his conscience, but finally he overcomes these urges and rededicates himself to indolence. It is an ironic echo of Christ's three temptations in the wilderness. The message of the poem would appear to be that at times it is more romantic to give in to a natural instinct than to be a slave to duty.

There are three figures in the poem (Love, Ambition and Poetry), who pass by three times. Three has always been a symbolic number in art and literature, deriving from its traditional use in the sources of Western culture, the Bible, classical mythology and medieval folklore: e.g. the trinity, the three Fates, the three Graces, the three bears, three wishes, three princesses. Three is a powerful number because it is not divisible and can therefore represent unity. It is also considered to be mystical and magical, especially when self-multiplied to become nine.

Language
The words from the ode which are typical of Keats' diction and themes are:

■ white	■ melt	■ wings	■ flowers	■ warmth
■ marble	■ faded	■ joy	■ vine	■ adieu
■ urn	■ burn'd	■ sweet	■ farewell	■ cool-bedded
■ ripe	■ ached	■ drowsy	■ shower	■ eyes
■ drowsy	■ pale	■ honied	■ lids	■ night
■ blissful	■ watchful	■ sleep	■ tears	■ store
■ pulse	■ fever-fit	■ dreams	■ budding	■ vanish

'Ode to a Nightingale'

This poem was written in 'two or three hours', according to Charles Brown (Wolfson, p. 90), in Hampstead in May 1819. Keats invented a new ten-line stanza for this ode, which he then used in the remaining three great odes.

The nightingale is an elusive bird famed for its beautiful but rarely heard sound. It is the bird of moonlit nights, associated with summer and romance. According to Greek mythology, the bird is the metamorphosis of Philomel, who was given a magical voice to compensate for having had her tongue cut out by her rapist, her brother-in-law Tereus, so that she could not accuse him or tell anyone of her ordeal.

Allusions
There are resonances in this ode of Spenser (deathwish), Milton (inspired blindness) and Ovid's Elegy III (Marlowe's translation includes 'as if cold hemlock I had

drunk'), and some critics see the influence, between lines 21–30, of Shakespeare's *Sonnet 73*. There are also echoes of *Romeo and Juliet* in the imagery of heaviness, poison and moonlight, and the failure of the young lovers to soar beyond the real world of age and conflict.

Narcotic diction

Keats' work is full of intoxicating substances, particularly the poppy derivatives opium and laudanum, which were commonly taken for alleged medical reasons. The heavy, drugged atmosphere of the first four lines is created by the words 'aches', 'drowsy', 'numbness', 'pains', 'hemlock', 'drunk', 'dull, 'opiate', 'sunk'. The rhythm of the opening, with its long vowels and **enjambement**, gives the effect of drowning in a narcotic haze. The repetition of the 'u' sound in 'numbness', 'drunk, 'dull', 'sunk', suggests the tolling of a funeral bell.

Mood swings

The ode is typical of Keats' characteristic mood swings. Paradoxically, the persona is in a depressed state and aching, though it is spring, because he is 'too happy' listening to the nightingale. The second half of the first stanza is much less heavy than the first; as soon as the nightingale is referred to in line 5 the pace increases and the diction becomes attractive and associated with lightness and joyful, unrestrained sound. 'Ease' in line 10 contrasts with the weightiness of the first half of the stanza.

The second stanza continues with the sensuous appeal of the south and the haunts of the gods, and the feeling of movement cancels the stasis and stagnation of the opening. Darkness ceases to be threatening and becomes romantic and enticing. However, there is another atmospheric shift in stanza three, back to cold harsh reality: pain, death and loss, and envy of the nightingale for having 'never known' 'the fever, and the fret' of the harsh conditions and 'human trammels' ('Lamia' I.210) to which thinkers, i.e. humans, are subject. Love and beauty are seen for what they are — temporary and disappointing.

Stanza 4 flies to a spiritual realm of imagination, beauty and light through poetry, but is brought back to earth in the last three lines, which stress the darkness and gloomy colours of mundane existence. But in the next stanza Keats compensates for lack of vision with the consolation of the sense of smell, though it is 'fast fading', and the sweet taste of fruit, and the satisfying sounds in the onomatopoeic line 'The murmurous haunt of flies on summer eves'.

There is a complete change of mood in the next stanza, which discusses the persona's death wish and burial. The transition back to the nightingale in stanza 7 releases a feeling of admiration and celebration of the bird's ancient lineage and romantic links with the biblical, classical and fairy-tale worlds, and with comedy and tragedy. The mood of the final stanza brings the poem to a melancholy conclusion.

The ending

The final stanza is worth detailed study to establish how its effects are achieved. There is an abrupt return to the present and the persona's awareness of himself, hinging on the repetition of the word 'Forlorn', which not only creates the idea of abandonment and loneliness, but reinforces the other funeral diction of 'anthem' and 'buried deep'. The persona realises that he does not have wings so cannot follow the nightingale and escape the constraints of being earthbound. The temporary flight by means of poetry has come to an end and he is reluctantly back in the physical world, his 'trip' or hallucination over.

The powerfulness of the experience triggered by the nightingale's song, the insecurity of the persona's life, and the deceiving nature of experience are all conveyed by the persona's need to ask whether he is awake or dreaming. Keats often crossed this physical and conceptual borderline to show the parallel existence of a dream world with different rules from the everyday. This allows him to make contrasts and evoke the moral dilemma of which world is preferable: is fancy being condemned as a dangerous delusion or is the poem celebrating the imagination for its ability to offer mortals a necessary escape route on the 'wings of Poesy' (line 33)? The question contributes to the mysterious atmosphere of the poem, magical sleep being a common feature of fairy tales. It adds to the characterisation of the persona as a daydreamer or somnambulist.

The **end-stopped** lines bring the poem back to a static state. The return gives the impression that the poem is framed by reality, enclosing a flight of fantasy; thought processes are circular and concerns do not go away, but they can be temporarily evaded through art. Dream, fantasy and illusion are, however, deceptive and unsustainable. The vision has faded, as all visions do, and left a sense of emptiness and absence (as in 'La Belle Dame sans Merci').

Ambiguities

The poem has been described as having rich ambiguities. Here are some of them:

- The nightingale, which is both woman and bird, is also both a real sound (Keats heard one on Hampstead Heath) and an abstract symbol of inaccessibility and immortality.
- The poet persona is playing two roles: creator of poetry and experiencer of the sublime, and suffering John Keats nursing his dying brother.
- He is 'too happy' and therefore in pain.
- Fancy is a cheat but also a necessity.
- Darkness is both threatening and magical, an oppression and a release.
- 'Fade away' has positive connotations of escape in lines 20 and 21, but a distressing one in line 75.
- The speaker is sometimes light and with the nightingale, and sometimes heavy and anchored to earth.

- The speaker may be awake or dreaming.
- Wine is summoned and then rejected in favour of 'Poesy'; i.e. the visible and physical is replaced by the intangible and invisible, but then that too is rejected.
- 'Embalmed' in line 43 means both preserved in death and fragrant, and is linked to 'incense' in line 42.
- The poet is only 'half in love with easeful death', which is presented as something to be desired rather than feared, though earlier in line 26 death is not an attractive prospect.

'Ode on a Grecian Urn'

This poem was written in April 1819, a very low point in Keats' life when he was tortured by lack of money, poor health, an unhappy love affair and a diminishing family. The ode includes reference to the standard rivalry between the sister arts, i.e. pictorial and verbal. Horace claimed that poetry is a speaking picture, and that painting is silent poetry. Here pictorial art is presented as cold artifice and contrasted to poetry, which represents warm passion. But it is not as simple as this; the ode contains ambiguities and complexities of meaning, including the reference to a 'legend', which normally refers to words but in this case to pictures.

The urn

Keats' urn is evidently funerary. No specific urn has been traced, but if it is made of marble, as appears to be the case, it must be neo-Attic; however, these urns have one circular scene going round the vase, whereas Keats' urn has two separate scenes.

This suggests the urn of the ode must be of his own invention. He was familiar with the classical world, including the Elgin Marbles — before which he used to sit rapt — and their Phidian sculpture, which is simpler than neo-Attic; scenes of Bacchic revelry are common on Greek marbles in the British Museum, and in Renaissance paintings; descriptions of rustic sacrifice and revelry occur in 'Endymion'. Keats refers to a Greek vase in a letter to his brother George in March 1819. In the house in Rome in which Keats died there is a tracing made by Keats, of the Sosibios marble urn, an exhibit in the Louvre, depicting an altar and all the characters he describes in the ode: men and women, a goddess, musical instruments, an animal to be sacrificed (Bowra, p. 129). Keats' urn seems to have been a conflation of two vases, as there is another vase in the Louvre with a flute-player, a nearly naked man pursuing a woman, and a vine pattern.

This ode is 'on' an urn, whereas in their respective odes the Nightingale, Autumn and Psyche are presented as living and the odes are therefore addressed 'to' them. The urn, like melancholy, is an abstract and is treated more distantly, as if the poet is giving a commentary on their existence or presence, a kind of academic lecture, but not having a dialogue with them, despite the rhetoric of addressing them. The essentially non-responsive, inanimate nature of the urn is therefore implicit in the title.

Language

Rhetoric

The poem contains many questions and exclamations; these rhetorical devices contribute to the tone and feeling of the poem, and its relationship with the reader. By employing interrogative and exclamatory modes the speaker is able to avoid declarative statements and convey uncertainty, passion, intimacy, and an openness to sensation and speculation, as well as a strong emotional engagement. Questions and exclamations create an illusion of spontaneity and a sense of flux; they also indicate the mood changes of the persona who is the voyeur on the reader's behalf, and represents the reader's likely responses. The asking of questions naturally leads to the provision of answers, thus establishing a dialogue between reader and persona.

The six questions in stanza 4 create a speeding up of pace to the climax of the frantic rhythm of Dionysiac frenzy. They are different from the questions in the first stanza, which are a device for describing the picture on the urn and showing the fascination of the viewer. They create a rhythm and mood opposite to the quietness of early lines such as the opening one, which stresses lack of movement and is a preparation for the calm reflectiveness and resolution of the final stanza.

Repetition

Another noticeable stylistic feature is repetition; e.g. in the third stanza the word 'happy' is used six times. The effect of this repetition is to convey a desperation of desire for and envy of happiness, with even a loss of control signified by a rare lapse into cliché. Perhaps the dimming of Keats' critical faculty is caused by personal trauma, since 'hectic' and 'feverish' are symptoms of his own tubercular disease. Walsh (p. 236) refers to a 'taint of sickness' permeating this stanza.

Fusions

The poem has been described as one of fusions, and these can be identified on many levels. The most notable synthesis is that between art and nature as represented by the existence (man-made) and decoration (pastoral) of the urn. Other fusions are those of men and gods, static and kinetic, timeless and temporal, mortal and immortal. It is addressed as both a fair maiden ('still unravished bride') and as a 'Sylvan historian' (presumably male). There is a fusion of observer and observed to the extent that there is debate about who is talking to us in the final lines. Its two sides fuse joyful and painful experience as one work of art, as does the poem.

Contrasts

Stillinger argued that 'There is a greater density of opposites in this poem than in perhaps any other of comparable length in all of English literature' (Wolfson, p. 255). The urn is sitting in a museum in a cold climate, depicting an outdoor scene in a hot country. Marble is synonymous with coldness and hardness, an ironic contrast to the passionate warmth of the depicted scene. It is solid and permanent, yet captures the

essence of the emotional and the spiritual; it is a presence denoting an absence, a living frieze of suspended action; a depiction of change in an eternal form. The two scenes are contradictory, one Dionysiac and one Apollonian, ecstacy and order, love and death.

The word 'still' in the first line is ambiguous (even as to whether it is an adverb or an adjective, according to whether Keats intended the comma which sometimes follows it) but all its adjectival meanings — unmoving, silent, permanent — are relevant to the properties of the urn. The first side depicts trees (nature), music (art) and lovers (spirit), symbolising a oneness of experience; in the third stanza there is perpetual movement but no change in love or nature or art, and therefore no threat of disenchantment or winter or end to the song. However, there is a turning, literally and metaphorically, of the urn between stanzas 3 and 4, indicated by the disturbing diction 'high-sorrowful', 'cloy'd', 'burning' and 'parching'. The urn rotates and introduces the melancholy note which is the undercurrent of all human happiness. It includes a scene of the imminent killing of an innocent victim for sacrifice; people who can never return home; desolate streets; the forlorn sound and pun of 'morn'. This prepares the reader for the 'woe' of the historical time of the final stanza and this 'other side' of the urn shows the dialectical progression of all experience on earth: joy followed by pain.

Paradoxes

Critics and readers have puzzled and argued for centuries over what the urn represents, since there are many paradoxes and therefore ambiguities inherent in the poem. The timeless rapture the ode describes is enjoyed by the participants on the vase, by the poet in his concentration on the urn, and by the reader absorbed in Keats' poem. The reader is therefore in a third level of engagement with beauty, admiring the ode as a masterpiece of creative ecstasy as much as Keats is likewise admiring the urn.

There are many further paradoxes in the poem. The urn is:

- a 'still unravish'd bride' — an oxymoron; the natural order is subverted by the museum context which keeps the urn and the maiden untouchable, inviolable and unchangeable in a glass case, but loved through many generations
- a 'Cold Pastoral' — an oxymoron linking art and death with nature and life
- an example of 'the supremacy of ideal art over nature, because of its unchanging expression of perfection' (Bridges, quoted in Bowra, p. 142), yet the subject of the perfect picture is a scene from nature that includes mutability and mortality
- depending on the poet as a medium of communication and the poet is depending on the urn as a creative inspiration for a poem
- kept in a quiet place where time is slow, but portrays speed and passion
- representing historical time but transcending it by making a single moment last for ever
- eternal yet fragile and vulnerable

- a permanent symbol of the impermanence of human activity
- a solid object and an 'ethereal thing' (letter to Bailey, March 1818) that is immensely old and forever new
- decorated with silent pipers — this alludes to the Elizabethan concept of the music of the spheres (planets), which cannot be heard by mere mortals
- both a reminder of the 'fever and the fret' of the world as well as a release from it
- a comment on reality but is itself a fiction
- a human creation which has outlived its creator, and may outlive all humanity
- inanimate clay addressed as a 'historian' and prophet
- a funeral urn celebrating life
- a heaven on earth or an earth in heaven
- here but otherworldly
- imbued with a musical quietness and a noiseless din

The urn shows us the limitations of our knowledge but tells us that there are none to our imagination. The final paradox is that although it represents 'silence', it has a message for us, and one in the form of an oracle, traditionally a gnomic and ambiguous utterance.

Who says the last 13 words?

There are three variant punctuations of the final lines in existence: Keats' own autograph, the version published in January 1820 in the magazine *Annals of the Fine Arts*, and the published volume of June 1820. Alternative meanings are created by moving or removing the inverted commas.

The final printed version, which most modern editions follow, was decided by John Taylor and Richard Woodhouse, who prepared the volume for publication and substantially altered the syntax and punctuation. It includes inverted commas, which do not appear in the two earlier versions (see Bowra, p. 145), implying either that the final two lines are the message of the urn, or that only five words are the message and the rest is Keats' opinion:

> 'Beauty is truth, truth beauty,' — that is all
> Ye know on earth, and all ye need to know.

The general critical view now is that the five words are in inverted commas because they constitute the motto, but that what follows is also the urn 'speaking', since Keats would probably not address the reader or mankind generally as 'ye'. The urn has more authority, as a voice from the 'other side', than Keats in this context, and it would be presumptuous and 'preachy' of him to assume the status of someone above the earthly realm. There has been no preparation for the direct address to the reader by the poet, who has addressed only the urn thus far.

However, the other reading is that, because it is not in inverted commas, it must be the poet who says 'that is all/Ye know...' and he is addressing the reader

as 'ye' to mean all humanity, and to distinguish from his addressing the urn as 'thou'. Keats has finished his lecture on the urn now, and is pointing the moral for the benefit of his audience.

Keats' original punctuation, though, allows for the possibility that he intended the voices of the urn and the poet to be fused in the final two lines as an instance of **negative capability**. Keats himself wrote:

> Beauty is truth, truth beauty, — that is all
> Ye know on earth and all ye need to know.

This suggests that the urn is speaking right to the end. Contemporary handwritten versions were the same. Keats, however, was not careful with punctuation and left it to his publishers. The version in *Annals of the Fine Arts* magazine also had no quotation marks, but changed the comma after 'beauty' to a full stop. This has the effect of separating the speaker of the aphorism (the urn) from the last 13 words. The version with inverted commas also has the effect of making the urn speak only the aphorism, leaving it to the poet as teacher to tell us that passion can reconcile the opposition between art and life.

The message

There are many possible interpretations of the message 'Beauty is truth', some of which are listed below.

(1) Garrod (Bowra, p. 146) interprets the lines as 'there is nothing real but the beautiful and nothing beautiful but the real'. Keats is using the word 'truth' to refer to a theory of art to explain his own experience as creator and viewer. This message is all the creative artist needs to know in order to continue to pursue and produce art.

(2) '[T]he discovery of beauty through the imagination is more satisfactory than the discovery of facts through reason' (Bowra, p. 147) and, paradoxically, more permanent. Aesthetic appreciation is more enduring and compelling, and less transient, than scientific beliefs. Inspired insight can pierce to the heart of things more keenly than abstract reasoning.

(3) Beauty is a synthesis of the temporal and atemporal worlds of reality and art, as symbolised by the fusion between the urn and its depiction.

(4) Beauty is true because it can be embodied in a permanent form, and the only thing which has lasting value in a transient world.

(5) Truth is perceived as beauty when the harmony of the human imagination with the object of its quest is attained.

(6) Beauty is truth because it is ephemeral, and this is the fundamental fact of life.

(7) Beauty is truth because it leads us to the border ('heaven's bourne', Wasserman, quoted in Bate, p. 12) which separates us from heaven but allows us a glimpse of it.

(8) Truth is normally associated with a religious revelation, and the beauty of the urn has provided this experience for the observer/worshipper.

(9) As with a solution to a maths problem, truth gives aesthetic satisfaction.

(10) In ancient philosophies wisdom (i.e. truth) was associated with beauty. Truth cannot be associated with ugliness, which connotes evil.

(11) Beauty is a fictional creation but fiction reveals universal truths.

(12) Art endows man's earthly existence with a meaning and a purpose.

(13) '[R]eality has become vicarious experience' (Wasserman, ibid., p. 124) now the poet has moved beyond the urn and into the life of its figures, with all distance removed so that art has become reality, beauty has become truth.

(14) 'The intention of the poem...must be to hold up art as the source of the highest form of wisdom' (Wasserman, ibid., p. 138), since it alters insight and inspiration.

(15) Truth can only be experienced empirically through the senses, through intense experience, not through statements of fact or proved propositions. 'I have never yet been able to perceive how anything can be known for truth by consecutive reasoning' (letter to Bailey, 22 November 1817).

(16) Truth is beautiful because of the miracle of our human faculty of being able to apprehend it.

(17) The search for truth is a mistaken human quest because knowing truths interferes with imaginative power (and **negative capability** is therefore the ideal state for the poet).

(18) What happens is by definition true and there is a beauty in the moment of recognition, however painful.

(19) The urn is a 'historian' whose job is to remind us of mortality, but this unpalatable truth is rendered beautiful by the artistry of the medium of communication.

(20) The urn is an unfathomable wonder, and a repository of knowledge and experiences beyond human range. We do not need to know the answers, but only to appreciate the beauty of the mystery.

(21) Horace was right: beauty (pictorial) and truth (verbal) are not distinct.

(22) Beauty is the only aspect of the human condition which can be universally agreed upon (unlike goodness, duty, morality, religion etc.) whereas in the presence of beauty all humans are awestruck.

(23) The Platonic philosophy was that beauty perceived on Earth is merely a pale reflection of the ideal beauty which can be directly apprehended, as the truth, only after death.

(24) 'What the imagination seizes as Beauty must be truth' (letter from Keats to Benjamin Bailey, 22 November 1817).

It could be concluded that although the **aphorism** sounds compelling, it 'really makes very little sense' (Stillinger, quoted in Wolfson, p. 256). Perhaps the problem is that Keats is trying to put into words something fundamentally inexpressible.

'Ode on Melancholy'

Influences
Melancholy was the favourite mood of the Romantic poets, connected by them to the season of autumn which is a visible sign of nature's transience and the passing of joy. It means pessimism and introspection (literally 'black bile'), even to the point of madness, and is therefore associated with mourning and depression (as Shakespeare used it in *Hamlet*). This ode shows the influence of Burton's *The Anatomy of Melancholy* (1621), Milton's 'Il Penseroso' (1632), and Gray's 'Elegy Written in a Country Churchyard' (1750). An earlier cancelled opening stanza contained Gothic description of bones and ships of death, similar to Coleridge's 'Rhyme of the Ancient Mariner', which gave the poem an even more macabre and medieval atmosphere. It was probably written in May 1819 and is shorter than the other odes.

Language and style
Deathly diction
The imagery in the first stanza derives from classical mythology and concerns the darkness and drugs that destroy consciousness or kill the body. There are many words which are reminders of death:
- 'Lethe' is the river of the Underworld whose waters induce forgetfulness
- 'Wolf's-bane' is a poisonous plant, and bane means 'cause of ruin'; the wolf is a fierce animal of prey and the death-dealing villain of many fairy tales
- 'poisonous'
- 'pale forehead', as of a corpse
- 'nightshade' is *Atropa belladonna*, the plant known as 'deadly nightshade', which has a toxic berry; the word shade also conjures up the ghostly inhabitants of the Underworld
- Proserpine was abducted, raped and kept imprisoned in the Underworld by Hades
- 'yew-berries' are poisonous, and the yew tree traditionally borders cemeteries
- 'beetle'; 'death-moth'; the 'owl' — three creatures associated with the eighteenth-century graveyard school of poetry and Gothic horror tales

Synaesthesia

In the second stanza Keats employs his characteristic device of synaesthesia. Four of the five senses occur in this stanza: 'glut', 'feed', 'globed', 'salt', 'rich' and 'rose' are synaesthesic in that they suggest more than one sense. Red is the sensuous and sensual colour suggested as the antidote to black melancholy.

Personification

The personifications of Joy, Beauty, Pleasure, Delight and Melancholy in stanza 3 introduce allegory to give the poem the classical element of being peopled with powerful and statuesque gods carrying symbols. Their physical poses reinforce the images of taste and ingestion which dominate this final stanza. The capitalisation of their names draws attention to the abstractions and their opposing qualities, some male and some female. The strong visual element created by the tableau of immortals is reminiscent of Renaissance allegorical paintings.

Meaning

The structure of the poem is dialectical and circular: it takes a stand against the seductiveness of oblivion, then a stand in favour of awareness, despite its drawbacks. The argument is that we should abandon our usual response to depression, which is a quest for death, or resorting to sedation which reduces one's perception and ability to feel.

Instead, we should deal with an attack of melancholy by turning to nature and her 'peerless' beauty, however fleeting, as a remedy, and shrug off the 'shroud' by appreciating the richness of life. Nature provides antidotes to the poisons. Thus one can become reconciled to Melancholy and be accepted as her devotee, subject to acceptance that pleasure inevitably turns to 'sadness' and that to enjoy the former you have also to be willing to experience the latter. The idea of sipping 'poison' in the last stanza returns the poem to the beginning.

In a modern idiom, the message of the poem is no gain without pain; or that one must brave the troughs of life if one wishes to enjoy the peaks. As usual, Keats has attempted a resolution, but it is worth noting that Milton could not reconcile 'L'Allegro' (the cheerful man) and 'Il Penseroso' (the melancholic man), presenting them in separate poems as two different human types and approaches to life. Keats is offering the partial consolation that experiencing melancholy, which is an intimation of mortality, brings a sudden increase of one's consciousness and appreciation of being alive, and therefore should be faced full on, not avoided.

But everything contains within it the seed of its own destruction: joy is fleeting, beauty must fade, and in the midst of life we are in death. The graveyard imagery is a **memento mori**: death will obliterate us in the end anyway, so there is no point in trying to resist Melancholy's sovereign power; we are her vanquished trophies. The final message is therefore a melancholy one.

'To Autumn'

This poem was composed on 19 September 1819 after a walk through the fields outside Winchester. Keats wrote in a letter to Reynolds on 21 September 1819:

> How beautiful the season is now — How fine the air. A temperate sharpness about it. Really, without joking, chaste weather — Dian skies — I never lik'd stubble-fields so much as now — Aye better than the chilly green of the Spring. Somehow a stubble-plain looks warm — in the same way that some pictures look warm — This struck me so much in my Sunday's walk that I composed upon it.

For once the English countryside on a particular day was Keats' inspiration, rather than a season-less classical landscape or an allegorical medieval one, which is perhaps why the poem is not called an ode like the other poems in the group.

The progress of the day, a miniature version of the progress of the season, is the chronological structure of the poem, which consists of a series of tableaux scenes of the labours of autumn, as in a medieval calendar of nature, which charts the process from reaping grain to gleaning it, from picking apples to seeing their 'last oozings' in the 'cyder-press'.

Language

Though the ode falls within the **georgic** tradition of Virgil and is classical to the extent that Autumn is personified, it is nonetheless without any Latinate Miltonic vocabulary (Keats had just decided to give up 'Hyperion' for that alleged reason) and favours diction from the domestic and agricultural register. It is possible to read the ode as a hymn of praise to the work of creation. Like its subject, it is short but full and compact.

Ripeness

The poem could be said to be a celebration of Shakespeare's line in *King Lear* that 'Ripeness is all'. Many words and phrases suggest the idea of maturity, in sound as well as associations of meaning. The colour scheme of the first two stanzas is a warm one of ripe fruit and autumn leaves: red, russet, gold, yellow, brown. The diction which is suggestive of ripeness is: 'mellow', 'fruitfulness', 'maturing', 'swell', 'plump', 'sweet', 'o'er-brimm'd', 'store', 'granary', 'oozings', 'cyder'.

Abundance

The effect of so many single and double 'l' sounds is one of luxuriance and happy excess. The 's' and 'z' sounds in the first stanza convey a feeling of ease and satisfaction deriving from the largesse of the fruitfulness.

The theme of the abundance and generosity of nature is conveyed by the content and form of the poem, as well as by its language:

- the irregular shape of the stanzas, with their staggered indented lines, suggests there is too much to be contained

- double letters: e.g. 'budding', 'summer' (lines 8 and 11)
- plural nouns throughout signify plenty
- repetition of the products described: corn, flowers, fruit
- **enjambement** for an effect of spillage
- vowel length: especially the long 'ee' of 'season', 'eves', 'trees', 'bees', 'cease', 'asleep', 'gleaner', 'keep'
- 'o'er-brimm'd' is a visualisation of the concept of excess
- semicolons represent a reluctance to come to a full stop and a preference for continuing a theoretically never-ending list, a cornucopia.

Heaviness

Walsh (p. 238) describes Autumn as having 'density and definition, weight and pressure', since many words and phrases give the impression of mass, shape and heaviness. As in a harvest festival or prize vegetable competition, size matters, as does shape: gourds are celebrated for their bottom-heaviness; 'load', 'laden', 'press' and 'crushed' convey the idea of pressure; the 'bend' of the apple trees and the rotundity and solidity of apples and nuts, seeds and cores suggest weight; 'plump' and 'swell' are verbs of size and shape; honey is dense and heavy; 'the fume of poppies' induces heavy-lidded drowsiness; sitting on the floor is collapsing under one's own weight. It is the heaviness of the grain which causes it to fall back to the threshing floor during winnowing, and therefore weight, as much as ripeness, is integral to the ritual of harvest, which is synonymous with autumn.

Autumn's gender

Autumn is **apostrophised** and **personified** in the poem, but there is disagreement about whether the figure is male or female. Sheats wrote that 'Autumn's gender [...] is left indeterminate, so that it is the reader who imagines it as male or female' (Wolfson, p. 97). Although many readers assume that the personification of Autumn is female, there is no absolute reason to do so, given that in 'Endymion' he is 'Autumn bold'. The seed-producing gleaner cutting swathes with a 'sickle' suggests masculinity by its association with seed and with death as the grim reaper. Traditionally, the season was presented in art as male. Flowing hair long enough to be 'lifted by the winnowing wind' (line 15) — often given as conclusive evidence for interpreting Autumn as female — was a feature of Apollo and other male Greek deities. Perhaps the word 'bosom' (line 2) conjures a female image, but the suggestion that he is a 'friend' of the male sun, rather than a lover, implies a male.

 An argument for Autumn being female is that other females in Keats are cruel or indifferent ('careless'), but then so are many of his masculine characters. The reproductive force, however, is essentially female, as in Ceres and Gaia and other earth goddesses, and this would provide a reproductive equation with the generically male sun, Apollo. In the same letter to Reynolds, 'Dian skies' associates autumn with the goddess Diana.

Change

'To Autumn' was written simultaneously with 'The Fall of Hyperion', and awareness of transience and loss is equally strong in both poems; no amount of divine or human conspiring can deflect inevitable change. The next change of season is signified in the ode by various means. In the last stanza the end of the day represents the end of the year (and the end of the human life span). The persona's perspective becomes distant and wide, to cancel the previous intimacy and close focus. Sentences shorten, and finite verbs multiply; the warm days are now ceasing. The imagery creates anticipatory tension and the expectation of approaching winter and coldness hangs over everything; the wildlife is aware of it. In the first two stanzas Autumn is suspended in passivity and indolence, but in the third there is a flurry of activity in preparation for winter or escape to warmer climes. The personification of the season has disappeared. Spring and summer are mentioned in the ode, so for the sake of completeness winter is also included.

Death

This ode is often considered to be Keats' most detached poem, yet it could also be one of his most personal, as there are reasons to think that death, or dying young, is an element in the poem. At the time this poem was written, Keats had pressing concerns about his own health and his brother was already dead. As a medical student he must have known the cause of his persistent sore throat and its likely consequence. He saw plenty of examples of early and horrific death at Guy's Hospital. In the same letter as quoted above, Keats told Reynolds: 'I always somehow associate Chatterton with autumn.' Thomas Chatterton was a poet who took his own life in despair in 1770 at the age of 17 and was regarded by Keats as a romantic icon and a victim of philistinism.

Perhaps the poem is an attempt to make some sense out of dying young, and even to beautify it. The verb 'to autumn' first appeared in the OED in 1771, so perhaps Keats dropped the word 'ode' from the title (which appears in the other five ode titles) to emphasise the active (for nature) and passive (for humans) process of maturing, ageing and dying.

The word 'dies' and related words and synonyms for finality are used throughout the poem: 'cease', 'asleep', 'hook', 'last', 'soft-dying', 'sinking'. The sounds in the last stanza are high-pitched and thin, in contrast to the low and mellow sounds of autumn (bees); 'wailful', 'choir' and 'mourn' conjure the sounds of a funeral dirge. The apples have been crushed and the lambs, full-grown but still young, await slaughter; 'sallows' are weeping willows (so-called in Spenser); stubble is all that remains after the cutting of the corn (which echoes Gray's 'Elegy', a similar poem in mood and content). 'Where are the songs of Spring?' laments the passing of youth, of Keats' brother Tom, of Chatterton, of unfulfilled artistic promise, and is a question reminiscent of the traditional cri de coeur 'Where are the snows of yesteryear?' ('*Où sont les neiges d'antan?*', François Villon, 1461), which calls attention to the loss of the past and the inevitable decline towards death. It is difficult not to see this poem as an elegy, though it begins as a **eulogy**.

The narrative poems

Keats' fans often enthuse about his longer poems and have a high regard for his ability as a narrative poet, though this is less evident in his earlier efforts. At his best, Keats employs a range of traditions and techniques to enhance characterisation, create tension and maintain reader interest. The most common are listed below and it is useful to have ready examples of each of them for use in exam essays:

- direct speech
- dialogue
- mystery
- suspense
- supernatural elements
- horrific sights
- emotional conflict
- physical violence

- surprising imagery
- exotic diction
- romantic location
- physical attractiveness
- detailed description
- irony
- ambiguity

'Endymion'

'Endymion' was the result of a contest between Keats, Hunt and Shelley as to who could write a 4,000-line poem within 6 months; Keats wrote this four-book epic between April and November 1817 and won. The poem asks 'Wherein lies happiness?' and it is generally assumed that it is a confessional poem (see Bush, quoted in Bate, p. 18) and that Endymion is John Keats. The poem is about the relation of the artist to his art, and to the world in general; it is a search for perfection and for the identity of the poet, written in the heroic couplets of epic verse.

Sources and inspiration

The plot is a recurring one in romantic literature and is the basis of Spenser's *The Faerie Queene*: the pursuit of an ideal love who has been glimpsed in a vision. The source of 'Endymion' is the Greek fable of the goddess Cynthia's love for a mortal shepherd on Mount Latmos, but Keats puts the emphasis on his love for her.

Keats related the story to Fanny in a letter of 10 September 1817 from Oxford, the city of dreaming spires. Cynthia visits Endymion in his sleep, and when he awakes he resolves to seek her — similarities to the plots of 'Lamia', 'The Eve of St Agnes' and 'La Belle Dame sans Merci'. On his quest Endymion falls in love with and shows pity to an Indian maiden, who turns out to be Diana. The moral is therefore that love for a mortal is the necessary compromise route for approaching the ideal. The hero, a beautiful dreamer, learns that the actual world of human life

must be accepted and that ideals can only be realised through participation and not withdrawal. Imagination and experience must therefore be fused and cannot exist fruitfully in isolation (see Lycius' argument in 'Lamia'). The dream goddess represents ideal beauty and therefore ideal love, linking the poem's philosophy to Platonism and the ideas expressed in 'Ode on a Grecian Urn' (see Bowra, p. 138). Humans must accept the fact of impermanence, i.e. mutability; Cynthia/Diana is the goddess of the moon, a symbol of inconstancy and flux.

The poem is dedicated 'To the memory of Thomas Chatterton', whom Keats honoured as 'The most english of Poets except Shakspeare'(sic), in a Preface to 'Endymion', rejected by his publishers. Keats was touched not just by Chatterton's tragic death — aged 17, alone and neglected in an attic in Holborn — but by his theme of mutability, which Keats was learning to embrace.

Reception

'Endymion' received a mauling by critics, who were scandalised by its sensuality when it was published in a separate volume in 1818. It was condemned as 'imperturbable drivelling idiocy' in a series of articles attacking the 'Cockney School of Poetry' in *Blackwood's Magazine* by a critic called Lockhart, who advised Keats to return to his apothecary's shop. This prejudice was attributable to the political bias of Tory supporters against the coterie of the anti-Tory Leigh Hunt, of which Keats was a member. But Keats himself expressed dissatisfaction with the technique and feeling of the poem as soon as it was finished, believing that he had not succeeded in embodying his principle, and that there was no accord between intention and outcome because of several factors: excessive ornament, unclear transitions, no clear plan and an effect of laxity.

Stylistic devices and set pieces

The epic genre allows Keats to use the full range of traditional rhetorical and other poetic devices, such as **personification**, to give the poem grandeur. In addition to the classical landscape setting, it is a characteristic of epic to contain such set pieces as the addressing of gods by humans and choral laments. The poem contains two set pieces: the Hymn to Pan (I. 232–306) and the Song of Sorrow (IV.146–290). They bring together the main themes, images and preoccupations of Keats' poetry: love and loss, nature and seasons, worship and melancholy. They both have a biblical style and a classical content reminiscent of Milton.

Pan was the god of nature who inhabited the Greek mountainside and played pipes. Being a satyr (bottom half goat), he was lecherous. Hymn to Pan was Keats' favourite passage in the work; it is a precursor to the later odes in being an **apostrophe** to a deity. In the Song of Sorrow the senses are evoked with the sounds of birds and the smells of vegetation, and the whole passage consists of a favourite device of cataloguing. The usual colour scheme of red and gold, contrasted with milky paleness, is employed (e.g. 'purple hue' I.195 and 'cold mushrooms' I.234).

Keatsian language

'Endymion' is 'fluent, facile, sweetly insipid' (Walsh, p. 227). Other descriptions of this poem used by the same twentieth-century critic are 'decorative', 'sketchy', 'vaguely structured', 'sensuous richness without point', 'mellifluous', 'trivial', 'impossible to take seriously'. Keats agreed with the criticism when he himself accused the poem of 'mawkishness', meaning excessive sentimentality. It is noteworthy that the word 'sweet' is used 81 times in this poem.

The extracts anthologised in selections of Keats' poetry are usually from Books I and IV. In Book I there are many examples of long 'ee' sounds, oxymorons, typical colours, and fruit imagery: 'shrilly mellow' (I.146); 'teeming sweets' (I.224); 'ripen'd fruitage' (I.253); 'poppied corn' (I.255); 'creeping strawberries' (I.257). The Cave of Quietude description in Book IV yields such characteristic examples as: 'melting ice' (IV.535); 'Happy gloom!' (IV.536); 'dreamless sleep' (IV.542).

Other examples from Book IV include **assonance**, **alliteration**, **synaesthesia**, 'transferred' **epithets**, temperature and farewell images: 'the ripe grape is sour' (I.35); 'I bid adieu to all' (I.141); 'faces all on flame' (I.201); 'breathless cups and chirping mirth' (I.236); 'velvet summer song' (I.297); 'Diversely ting'd with rose and amethyst' (I.386); 'warm with dew at ooze from living blood!' (I.667); 'scarlet berry cups of dew' (I.674); 'his first soft poppy dream' (I.786).

'Isabella; or The Pot of Basil'

The three short narratives 'Isabella', 'The Eve of St Agnes' and 'Lamia' — as well as the odes and the two 'Hyperion' poems — were published in the 1820 volume of Keats' poetry. As with the other romance poems, this one calls attention to historical movement between cultural periods by making the claim 'Still is the burthen sung' in the penultimate line ('Upon a time' is the opening of 'Lamia', and 'ages long ago' the ending of 'The Eve of St Agnes'). It is written in 63 stanzas of Italian **ottava rima**, i.e. eight iambic lines containing three rhymes, arranged as ab, ab, ab, cc. This has been criticised as an inappropriately light stanza form for such a grisly tale.

Sources and influences

The poem's source is Boccaccio's *Decameron*. It tells of the Florentine lovers, Isabella and Lorenzo, who cannot be married because Isabella's brothers consider Lorenzo socially inferior and are greedy for a rich brother-in-law. They murder Lorenzo in a forest and lie to Isabella about his whereabouts. She learns in a dream where to find Lorenzo's body, and when she does, she removes his head and plants it in a pot of basil. She keeps it in her room, where it flourishes so amazingly that her brothers discover her secret and take away the head. They then run away from Florence, and Isabella dies of grief. The poem has similarities with 'The Eve of St Agnes' in having passionate lovers, vicious kinsmen, a trusty aged nurse, a crucial dream and a Renaissance setting.

Sweet basil is now a culinary (and sometimes medicinal) herb widely used in the Mediterranean, but was previously associated with burial rituals and graves in various countries. In Italy a pot of basil on a windowsill is meant to signal a lover; it is also conversely associated with chastity, and therefore with both love and death. Ancient Romans and Greeks believed that it represented hate and misfortune, and in modern-day Crete it symbolises 'love washed with tears'. Significantly it has a wonderful smell and taste, and dies every autumn.

Fairy tales

The poem includes typical fairy-tale elements. The characters are fairy-tale stereotypes: siblings without parents; identical brothers; poor suitor for a rich girl; imprisoned maiden in distress; faithful servant; family feud. The typical plot elements are forbidden love; being lured into a forest; a dream revealing the whereabouts of something hidden; sudden disappearances; a desire for riches; a secret solace; spying.

Horror

The poem also has characteristics typical of horror stories. The atmosphere of the poem is one of isolation, seclusion and solitude. The story not only includes two deaths but has many macabre elements: ruthless murder; a hidden grave in a forest; the ghost of Lorenzo; exhumation and decapitation; the nursing of the head; the flourishing of the basil. The churchyard description and religious references are characteristic of Gothic literature. Horror stories typically end with the exile of the villain.

Commerce

The poem makes use of the concept of triangulated desire (see Cox, quoted in Wolfson, p. 58) whereby the love affair is always mediated through fictional expectations and dream wishes, or the competition, interference or influence of others. The main mediating triangulation and threat to love in this poem is the spirit of commerce, which is antithetical to the spirit of love. Through the brothers and their behaviour to others, Keats is attacking the values of a money-mad society: capitalist exploitation and its corrosive effect on families and relationships; the diminishing of women because they do not have a public role; the damage caused by the deadly sins of pride and avarice.

Reception

Having completed the poem in Teignmouth in April 1818, immediately after 'Endymion', Keats recognised the adolescent sentiment in 'Isabella', and the incongruity between the horrible content and a sentimental tender prettiness. He said there was 'too much inexperience of life and simplicity of knowledge in it', and described it in the same letter to Woodhouse in September 1819 as 'too smokeable', meaning easily made fun of. Certainly this earlier narrative poem is not as complex as 'The Eve of St Agnes' or as ironic as 'Lamia', both of which are preferred by most modern critics and readers.

'The Eve of St Agnes'

This poem of early 1819, which is in the form of **Spenserian stanzas**, is considered Keats' most successful short narrative poem. Described as 'a decorative romantic experience' (Hough, p. 167) and 'a fairy-tale romance, unhappily short on meaning' (Stillinger, quoted in Bate, p. 72), it was inspired by Fanny Brawne at the beginning of Keats' relationship with her, when he was still healthy and hopeful of love and life. Perhaps because of this, it sympathises with lovers in revolt against a restrictive society and is the only one of the three romances which does not end in their death. The original stanza 36 was rejected by Keats' publisher because of its shocking suggestiveness; the replacement is more **euphemistic** but still overtly sexual.

Sources and influences

The legend of the Eve of St Agnes was that a maiden going supperless to bed on 20 January would dream of her future husband. Madeline does so, although there is a party going on in her father's castle. The mysterious Porphyro manages to gain access to her bedroom, with the help of her nurse, Angela, so that he is present in the flesh as well as in Madeline's dream. After their lovemaking, Madeline agrees to elope with him and they escape undetected.

There are echoes of Shakespeare's *Romeo and Juliet* in this poem. The most obvious similarities are the feuding families, the doom-laden atmosphere, the conflict between generations, the dangerous visit to forbidden territory and the maiden just reaching maturity, all of which are direct parallels with the situation in Verona; the grand setting in the home of the heroine, the nurse's collusion with the hero, and the inclusion of a party also link the two works. The bawdy and garrulous Angela is obviously based on Juliet's Nurse (named Angelica), and the Beadsman is an elderly and celibate religious figure like the Friar. There are many references to religion and worship in both works, and both contain recurrent imagery of tombs and darkness. However, Keats decided to give his work a happy, if vague, ending rather than a tragic one.

Lovers and dreamers

Love and dreams are the two main and intertwined strands of the poem, which is permeated by a sensuous happiness at odds with the poems written later in the same year. The later poems suggest that an individual ought not to lose touch with the realities of this world through idealisation and imagination, and the dreamers in these poems learn a hard lesson and either wake up to disappointment or come to grief through continuing to live in a fantasy. This poem, on the other hand, seems to suggest that a dream, if believed in and desired deeply enough, can turn into reality. However, this is a physical as well as a spiritual poem, and one which is pictorial and full of objects and precise descriptions.

Temperature

The first four stanzas establish the images of coldness used throughout the work, and it is clear that the reader is expected to associate them with age and religion, so that later a contrast can be made with youth, warmth and love, all connected with each other and associated primarily with the fiery Porphyro.

The colours used for the older generation are the lifeless ones of grey ashes and icy whiteness. The anonymous 'ancient Beadsman', who dies at the end of the poem, counts on his rosary and says prayers for the next world, unmindful of this one. Frozen and already sensually dead, he is cut off from feeling and represents the antithesis to the passion of erotic love. He is also the opposite of the 'Hyena foemen', who are guilty of wrath, violence, greed and selfishness, but his way of life is presented as equally barren. Madeline's bedroom, described as a cold chapel, is a parallel to the Beadsman's crypt below, until she is rescued from her state of virginity and it turns into a warm love-nest.

Feast

The poem is famous for its description of the feast in stanzas 29–31. With roots in classical literature, the Bible and folklore, the preparation of a feast is always a highly-charged symbolic rite and important for the creation of atmosphere at climactic moments. Shakespeare's comedies end with a feast to convey a feeling of relief and harmony.

This feast in the poem, immediately preceding the deflowering of the saintly Madeline, is notable for the richness of the contents and the sense of taste evoked, in combination with other senses, through the mention of aromas and strong red colours. It has been prepared for by the line 'Upon the honey'd middle of the night' (line 49), which is a typically Keatsian use of a taste adjective in a surprising context for the effect of forbidden pleasure, connecting sex, darkness and mouths/eating. (The line in Shakespeare's *Measure for Measure*, 'Upon the heavy middle of the night' (IV.1.34), is marked in Keats' copy; his change makes the metaphor more original and sensual.)

The feast has Middle- and Far-Eastern elements: exotic fruits and spices, such as 'dates', 'cinnamon' and 'cedar'; the precious substances of 'gold', 'silver' and 'jet'; the textures of wood, stone, silk and metal. The place-names mentioned are associated with deserts and biblical journeys. The smells, sights and tastes of the delicacies from a hot climate are in ironic contrast to the chasteness of the 'chilly room' and the sleeping girl in her herb-fragranced white linen. It is an idealised meal in that it consists entirely of sweets, mostly in the form of candied fruit; it is a children's party fantasy, an Arabian Nights meal, and heavenly manna all rolled into one; food fit for gods. Its preparation is an act of worship at the altar to Madeline. She herself is treated as a 'spiced dainty' (she shares her name with a sweet biscuit) and is the object of the consummation, also lying on a white cloth ready to be touched and tasted.

The feast represents everything that the hot youth Porphyro has to offer his cloistered virgin, and the joys of life in the warm south. It is of magical origin in two senses, given that no convincing explanation is given of how it all gets into the bedroom closet. He adds the playing of an instrument and singing of a ballad to complete the suite of sensations (and to continue the references to a wide range of sounds in the poem). The feast is after all left untouched, as if, after their union, they are no longer mortal and therefore do not require earthly sustenance. Edibility, not the eating, is its point; like the taking of virginity, the attraction lies in the anticipation. The reader/watcher is also having his or her taste buds teased by this fantasy feast. Trilling describes how 'the whole paraphernalia of luxurious felicity, the invoked warmth of the south, the bland and delicate food, the privacy of the bed, and the voluptuousness of the sexual encounter, are made to glow into an island of bliss with the ultimate purpose of making fully apparent the cold surrounding darkness' (Ricks, p. 123).

Porphyro: demon or saviour?

As usual there are ambiguities in the poem, particularly concerning the character of Porphyro. Stillinger claims there are 59 theoretical interpretations of 'The Eve of St Agnes' (Wolfson, p. 257), but two will do. Porphyro is presented throughout with the imagery of fire and his name means 'purple'; he could be bringing the life-giving heat of passion to Madeline, or coming to prey upon her. He is either a pilgrim at the altar or an infidel in the citadel.

The first interpretation is that Porphyro is the bold, charming and handsome romantic hero who is determined to win his lady and rescue her from imprisonment by unloving relatives and from the deadening company of ancient servants. He offers her love, freedom and a lifetime of devotion in the warm south. He is a crusading knight who frees a Christian maiden from heathens and who saves a 'lamb' from 'wolves and bears'.

The alternative is that Porphyro's seduction of Madeline is reminiscent of Satan's clandestine viewing and later seduction of Eve in the Garden of Eden. Like the serpent, he is sly and persuasive. Having chosen a night when he knows maidens are vulnerable, he schemes with Angela to gain access to Madeline, using the traditional tools of pathos and emotional blackmail (the threat of self harm) to gain entrance to the chamber, and the magician's trick of conjuring a fantasy feast. He takes advantage of Madeline's vulnerability to despoil her to satisfy his lust. In effect, he not only violates her, but his rape leaves her no alternative but to run away with him. His singing of 'La belle dame sans mercy' is a clue that Madeline will never awake from the blissful spell which he is casting over her. He is a demon who visits chaste maids' beds and couples with them (as the devil was thought to do). There are many references to demons as well as to a 'stratagem', and even Angela denounces him as a 'cruel', 'impius', 'wicked' deceiver.

Madeline: hoodwinked or rescued?

Madeline is portrayed as a saint, an angel ('seraph') in her own right, and as one of St Agnes' white lambs and sacrificial victims. She is also a defenceless bird; the poem is full of bird imagery: 'affrighted Swan' (i.e. about to die); 'ring-dove' (i.e. tamed); 'tongueless nightingale' (i.e. violated — see the mythological story of the rape of Philomel); a 'dove forlorn' (i.e. abandoned); a caged nightingale (i.e. imprisoned).

Stillinger's 'The Hoodwinking of Madeline' (Bate, p. 71) is an influential article which argues that Porphyro is in effect a 'peeping Tom and villainous seducer' and can only be said to be on a spiritual pilgrimage if 'the poem is to be read as a satire on spiritual pilgrimages'. His behaviour differs from Romeo's in that Juliet was a conscious and willing partner in all stages of their relationship. Like the Beadsman, Madeline set herself apart from actuality and other humans and dedicated herself to religious ritual, which is dangerously alienating. Like the knight in 'La Belle Dame sans Merci', also a religious figure, she is 'Hoodwink'd with faery fancy' (line 70) — adherence to one mystical system laying her open to the seductions of another. Stillinger sums up his argument: 'Porphyro is cruel; Angela is a traitor; and Madeline is a "deceived thing".' Angela (who is no angel) gives support to Porphyro, knowing his intention, which is tantamount to inviting evil over the threshold and giving it a welcome.

There is a long literary tradition, utilised by Shakespeare, of the young virgin being a challenge to the hot-blooded male. Porphyro's call for a sleeping potion (stanza 29) (the ancient equivalent of a date-rape drug) is reminiscent of the stratagem by which the rake Lovelace robbed Clarissa of her virginity and her life in Richardson's **eponymous** eighteenth-century novel. Like Satan in *Paradise Lost*, Porphyro is abashed by the beauty of his intended victim and has a moment of conscience before heartlessly proceeding to corrupt her and claim his conquest. Like Eve, Madeline makes the traditional lament of the seduced maiden, expressing an expectation of being abandoned and being sentenced 'to fade and pine'. The response by nature to the sexual act is reminiscent of that in *Paradise Lost* to the Fall and the loss of Eve's chastity. The consequences were not good.

On the other hand, Madeline's life does not seem particularly attractive, and she has no one she can trust or love. It is possible to claim that Madeline is the conjurer and initiator of the evening's entertainment, and has summoned Porphyro to fulfil her erotic desire and dream of escape. Porphyro gets into Madeline's warm bed, and into Madeline's warm body, during a storm, so that the cold, frosty wind and sleet of the outside world heighten the sense of the attractive cosiness within.

The end

Depending on one's view of Porphyro and Madeline's situation, one reads the ending of the poem differently. The lovers perhaps go off to a viable existence in the Mediterranean — 'southern' always meant the warm, poetic, classical Greece and Italy about which Keats was passionate. One must remember that he probably saw himself as Porphyro and Fanny Brawne as Madeline.

On the other hand, they could be seen as phantoms (either metamorphosed by love or because the vampire Porphyro has carried Madeline into his night-time world) in the 'elfin-storm from faery land' with 'sleeping dragons all around', unregistered by all but the dog (which typically has a supernatural sense). They have left the real world behind to cross into unchartered demon territory, like the ghostly knight in 'La Belle Dame sans Merci'. There is a suggestion that Madeline has not woken up, and may never do so if Porphyro has stolen her soul along with her body.

However, the last words of the poem make the fates of all the other characters seem worse: nightmares of death or death itself. We are then told that this story is an ancient legend of 'ages long ago', as if Keats is exonerating himself from responsibility for the outcome and giving the impression that the whole thing was a fairy story from start to finish, despite the descriptive detail. As in all romances, whether the outcome is comic or tragic, the external world invades the exotic retreat in the end; the only alternative to a return to reality is an escape to a completely different world.

'La Belle Dame sans Merci'

Sources and influences

Keats wrote two poems (the other being 'Lamia') with arguably bad, beautiful women as main characters, who are different from the more passive and conventional maidens of the earlier narratives — Isabella and Madeline — and could be said to have a vendetta against men and a desire to be in control. Written on 21 April 1819, this poem is reminiscent of the nightmarish dream sequences of Spenser's *The Faerie Queene* and has the typical medieval flavours of chivalry, thwarted love and supernatural characters. The title comes from an early fifteenth-century French poem written in the courtly love tradition, which is based on the convention that a mistress should accept graciously a knight's pleas of love and willingness to serve her. The Beautiful Lady without Mercy is, however, a stereotype of the femme fatale, the seductive enchantress who leaves men desolate and captivated, doomed to a lifetime of questing for the unattainable. French was the language of love and of the nobility in Britain after the Norman Conquest in 1066. It was (and still is) regarded as a more exotic and erotic language than English, and gives the lady a tantalising foreignness, as well as anonymity to represent her belonging to another world.

Mysteries

The poem is a ballad in quatrains of **iambic tetrameter** with a final half line. The unexpected shortness of the fourth line creates the effect of a truncated experience and of something lost or absent (compare the unusually long last line of the stanzas of 'The Eve of St Agnes', in which nothing is withheld). The first three stanzas are spoken by the questioner, the rest by the knight. The use of two voices is

characteristic of ballads, originally an oral genre, and creates not just the spontaneity of a dialogue but a question and answer structure. The unidentified questioner provides a framework and turns the poem into a dramatic encounter between two mysterious and anonymous male characters. The questioner represents the reader, who wants to know why the knight looks so 'pale' and distressed.

As usual in Keats, there is some ambiguity about what exactly has happened. The knight may have fallen asleep in the 'Meads', in which case he then has a dream within his dream, a nightmare within his idyll, in which he is warned about the Lady. He then either wakes from the inner dream but is still trapped in the original vision, like the other victims in the warning dream which came too late, or he is returned to where he was before he 'met a Lady', i.e. loitering by the lake, but not able to leave the place or adjust to the cold empty real world which contrasts too painfully with the summery fantasy of heavenly delights and satisfied senses. In either case, the questioner is the intermediary and this poem has a double crossing of the border between the everyday world of the knight and his two visions, one within the other. The use of a medieval setting transports the reader first into a bygone historical age and then into a fairy-tale world.

Absence

The first stanza uses imagery and diction which both create an atmosphere and suggest the state of the knight. The landscape portrayed is one of desolation, a wasteland from which all life has departed, which matches the pallor and doomed situation of the knight. The fact that 'no birds sing' stresses an absence of sound, and the stanza is also devoid of colour and movement. The words 'ail', 'alone', 'palely', 'withered' and 'no' denote absence and loss, illness and winter. The change of description of the sedge in the final stanza to 'is wither'd' rather than 'has withered' makes it an adjectival rather than a verb form, which makes the withering seem permanent.

Nature

The nature imagery elsewhere in the poem is also significant. The lily is the white flower of death, and it has chased out the rose from the knight's cheeks, i.e. warmth, blood and life have departed (the reverse transition occurs in 'The Eve of St Agnes') and left him stranded on the 'cold hill's side'. The smells of flowers and 'pacing', and all other senses and movement, belong to the blissful, magical world and are not present in the framework location. The images of taste are important in the creation of the erotic fantasy: 'sweet', 'honey', 'manna' and 'kisses'.

The word 'wither' is used three times, and applies to the knight as well as to the wintry vegetation; it contributes largely to the desolate mood of the poem. The knight has become fused with the landscape and we get the impression he will never be able to leave it. The 'return' technique of the ending gives the impression that the knight is perpetually trapped in a limbo between inaccessible fantasy and unacceptable reality. The lack of punctuation in the final stanza, compared to the first, deadens the tone; this in conjunction with the fact that the speaker has changed makes the external and mental states seem both mournful and final. It is as difficult to believe that spring will return to the meadows as it is that health and happiness will return to the knight.

Sympathy

It is possible either to sympathise with the knight or to despise him. One's first response is probably to see him as a helpless victim of the wiles of women or the machinations of an evil spirit, and his lonely 'haggard' state seems pitiable. He is both hopeless and helpless and as such seems to deserve reader sympathy, especially as many kings and princes, his social superiors, have also fallen under the spell of the 'faery child'. The fact that all the characters mentioned in the poem are male other than La Belle Dame builds up antipathy towards her for her sadistic treatment of men and the Gothic horror she inflicts. Some critics have suggested that the knight's banishment from female love, warmth and succour is an allegory of Keats' rejection at an early age by his mother, from which he may never have recovered. La Belle Dame may also be Fanny Brawne, from whom Keats was unable to 'wean' himself.

However, there were strict codes of conduct applicable to medieval knights — who vowed to uphold Christian values — which included their having to be ever vigilant against evil and its subtle disguises. One could therefore see the knight as having lost his virtue by being unable to resist the temptation of the woman with the 'wild, wild eyes'. There are parallels in *The Faerie Queene*, in which the Red Cross Knight is nearly fatally deceived by Duessa, who has a beautiful exterior but is ugly and evil beneath. The knight's dallying in an 'elfin grot' is an abdication of duty as an upholder of social and moral order, and it has rendered him useless as both a defender of the faith and a member of society. A psychoanalytical critique might say that the knight, epitome of masculinity as a warrior, is suffering from the guilt of having subjugated himself to a female and of having given way to forbidden sexual desire. The questioner seems to find his 'ailing' behaviour unusual and disturbing, rather than pitiful, and does not offer any sympathy after learning the cause of the knight's plight. Once again, the question of whether the dreamer figure is to be encouraged or condemned is being raised by Keats: is it better to have dreamt and lost, or never to have dreamt at all?

'Lamia'

Sources and influences

'Lamia' was written in 1820. Keats used **heroic couplets** to create an epic and classical effect consistent with its setting in Ancient Greece and the inclusion of mythological figures, though Keats' vision of Greece is partly 'medievalised' here. The poem tells the story of a young man of Corinth who unknowingly falls in love with a snake woman and insists on marrying her, despite her warning, and consequently

loses both her and his own life when his teacher challenges and exposes her at the wedding reception. A lamia is a fabulous monster with the body of a woman, who was said to prey upon human beings; in the Middle Ages witches were called *lamiae*, and this poem is partly 'medievalised'. Keats' contemporary Samuel Taylor Coleridge also used a lamia in his poem 'Christabel'. Keats found the story in Burton's *Anatomy of Melancholy*. Other sources and influences for this poem are the Bower of Bliss section in Spenser's *The Faerie Queene*, *Archaeologia Graeca* by John Potter, Ovid's *Metamorphoses*, and *The Life of Apollonius* by Philostratus.

Reception

The poem is technically impressive and a more structured narrative than its predecessor, 'Endymion', which was attacked by critics for being sprawling, among other things. This poem was also criticised, however, and in particular accused of having a cockney style of pretentious coinages and compounds, e.g. 'cirque-couchant' (line 46). Keats was aware that it would not please everyone, and wrote in a letter to George and Georgiana Keats on 18 September 1819: '...there is that sort of fire in it which must take hold of people in some way — give them either pleasant or unpleasant sensation.' Modern readers do not care for it as much as Keats himself did. The twentieth-century critic Graham Hough describes 'Lamia' as a 'rather purposeless poem' and no more than an 'exercise in verse-narrative'.

Framework

The opening of the poem to line 145 is Keats' original contribution to the story he found in *The Anatomy of Melancholy*. This section is often ignored or dismissed by readers and critics, though there must be a purpose to Keats' inclusion of the relationship between Hermes and the Nymph, and of the dialogue between Hermes and Lamia.

The human world is excluded from the framework story, and this acts as a contrast and warning that though affairs between gods and nymphs are possible, those between humans and gods are not; the mortal world is a place where the pursuit of desire is an illusion and where love fades. A feminist critique could see the god's unwanted pursuit of a friendless and vulnerable woodland nymph as an instance of sexual exploitation and abuse of power by a predatory male. That Lamia is willing to betray a fellow female and sacrifice her to the lascivious clutches of Hermes for her own benefit might suggest that her character is not wholly admirable, or conversely that her love for Lycius is genuine and overwhelming. What is certain is that the opening scene gives Lamia the status of a supernatural being, and a secret past which she keeps from Lycius.

Eyes

One of the striking aspects of the poem is the imagery of eyes. Traditionally eyes mesmerise, bewitch, turn to stone, are blind, love at first sight, show desire, lead to temptation, cast the evil eye, feast themselves, represent light, close in the blissful intimacy of 'slumberous repose' ('Bright star!...'). They are considered a human's most vulnerable point, and a window to the soul. Sinister humans and animals of prey (snakes, cats of all sizes, eagles) have intimidating eyes. The climax of the poem is the battle of the eyes, and therefore of the wills, of Lamia and Apollonius.

Transformations

'Lamia' is a story of transformations. Here are some of them:

- the invisible nymph becomes visible
- Lamia metamorphoses from serpent to beautiful woman — she claims to Hermes that she has been a woman already (line 117), so this is a retransformation
- Lycius the scholar becomes a lover
- a lengthy journey becomes short
- a humble house becomes a sumptuous palace
- Lycius changes from grateful slave to possessive master
- Lamia becomes a bride
- Apollonius, the teacher and friend, becomes an uninvited guest
- a noisy party becomes deathly quiet
- Lamia disappears, becoming 'a shade'
- Lycius, the groom, becomes a corpse

Lamia

Keats has left the issue of Lamia's identity and motives ambiguous and unresolved. His complicated feelings for Fanny Brawne may have influenced his presentation of Lamia: 'Ask yourself my love whether you are not very cruel to have so entrammelled me, so destroyed my freedom' (1 July 1819). Letters to her during this period show the same emotional tone as the poem; he is unable to wean himself from her and resentful of her power over him: 'You have absorbed me' (13 October 1819). Lamia's character and role can also be seen in both positive and negative terms.

Lamia is beautiful, in love, and deserves to be loved. She desperately tries to keep her lover but is destroyed by the cold and calculating Apollonius, killer of beauty, sensuousness and rainbows. Lamia previously crossed to the human world in her dreams and fell in love with Lycius in a reverse-gender parallel to the situation in 'La Belle Dame sans Merci'. If we are sorry for the knight in that poem, we should therefore have sympathy for Lamia, who did not choose to be trapped in the body of a snake and was willing to sacrifice her immortality for Lycius' sake. She represents the creative imagination, being able to transform invisible into visible and to satisfy desire; her kiss has the power to transport the chosen one to immortal bliss. If Lycius had not been so insistent on showing her off to arouse envy in his friends, both of them would have survived; therefore their demise is his fault, not hers. Like the nymph desired by Hermes, she is a passive object of the masculine drive to make conquests and possessions of desirable females; it is Lycius and Apollonius who cause the fatal outcome because of their own power struggle.

The alternative view is that she is a devious enchantress comparable to La Belle Dame, and like her a shifting evanescent creature always likely to disappear; or she is a Circean imprisoner of men whom she keeps to satisfy her own unwholesome lust. She is the active force in the poem, the one who changes and causes change in others, and who ruins the good relationship between teacher and pupil. The misogynistic Christian view, perhaps represented by Apollonius, was that all women, as descendants of the wicked temptress Eve, who caused the Fall of Man and was the prototype of the femme fatale, were deceivers and seducers in league with Satan, and therefore honorary serpents.

Apollonius

Apollonius is a historical character, half philosopher/half magician, who lived in the early Christian era. He signals a shift from classical/pagan to Christian which could be an allegorical interpretion of the poem as a whole: new male-dominated religion replaces earlier female pagan power. Apollonius the teacher/philosopher can be seen as either:

(a) a champion of truth and a seer with clear vision. He dedicates himself to saving his pupil's soul from the possession of an evil spirit which has cut him off from reality and must be exorcised. Like his divine namesake Apollo, he represents enlightenment and the truth of the sun as opposed to the deceptions of darkness and the shadowy moonlit world.

(b) a representative of cold science and destructive rationality. He is a murderer of youth and wonder, beauty and passion, who does not know or care about the ultimate ideal of love, being anti-sensual and anti-mystery; he reduces the sublimity of the rainbow to the 'dull catalogue of common things' (II.233) since 'all charms fly/At the mere touch of cold Philosophy' (II.229–30).

In this poem Apollonius provides the triangulation and mediating factor in the romance of Lycius and Lamia (see Cox, quoted in Wolfson, p. 60). It is perhaps useful to see him as an equivocal Ancient Mariner figure, who gatecrashes the party and destroys the mood, fixing guests with his steely eye. He is also a dutiful burster of fantastic bubbles and bringer of unpalatable but necessary home truths and **eternal verities**. A psychoanalytical approach to a reading of the poem would see Apollonius as a projection of the guilt of Lycius or as a voice of conscience warning of the consequences of unrestrained passion and the failure to reconcile the private world with the demands of a public one.

Love

Part II (lines 1–8) begins with an **interpolation** (typically Chaucerian) on the subject of love, but the poet declines to give a clear view. He notes the claim that love cannot survive painful reality, such as poverty, but that love 'in a palace' may, in the end, be worse (because of the jealousy of others). He appears to distance

himself from these views — 'a doubtful tale from faery land' — and then undermines this by implying that only the 'non-elect' (a revealingly elitist phrase, with overtones of Calvinism) would have difficulty in understanding it. Had Lycius lived, he might have cast some light upon this conundrum, but as he did not, Keats is reserving his position, though the interpolation proves that he felt personally and passionately on this subject. The passage reveals that Lycius is going to die and therefore introduces an atmosphere of doom to counteract that of bliss, making clear that pleasure has to be paid for with pain.

The general treatment of love in the poem is contradictory. It is: all-consuming; leads to excess; a snare and a delusion; an obsession; makes you blind; a short-lived excursion into the land of fantasy; a selfish pursuit causing the betrayal of friends and 'trusty guides'; an unhealthy self-gratification of the senses; a cause of character change for the worse. It is also, however: a transcendental experience; it enables one to see old things in new and improved ways; a transport to the ranks of the elect; a heavenly state; the only thing worth having; a precious gift under threat from the uninitiated, the uninvolved or the jealous.

The two Hyperion poems

An unfinished poem, or fragment, was a viable form for Romantic poets of both the first and second generation (Coleridge produced and published several). Since the Romantics regarded tinkering of any kind, and continuing when inspiration had departed, as artistic crimes, there was no shame attached to the failure to complete a work. What Keats' two unfinished versions have in common is that Hyperion, god of poetry, is the last of the twelve Titans to fall and this tenacity is a tribute to the endurance and supremacy of the spirit of poetry. Keats wanted to move on to a grand epic theme in the tragic mode of Milton and Shakespeare and to move away from the florid pastoral style of 'Endymion'. This story combined the magnificent passions and vast scale of Greek mythology with the complex relationship between mortality and immortality, as well as having a role for Apollo, god of the sun and poetry, thereby satisfying all of Keats' interests. He pondered on the subject for a long time before he began working on it. However, some critics have noted that the whole enterprise was contrary to the spirit and development of Romantic poetry, being based on epic objectivity rather than the personal and the spontaneous.

'Hyperion. A Fragment'

The first version Hyperion poem was started in autumn 1818 and abandoned in April 1819. Being mythological and pictorial, it demonstrates Keats' interest in statuary, primarily the Elgin Marbles. Like them, the poem is mostly façade, sculptural friezes, tableaux, and no action; in fact, it could be said to be smothered

under decoration. The narrative suffers from abrupt transitions and ineffective inter-weaving. The poem stops because Keats did not know how to go on; inspiration failed him. Ricks refers to its sudden ending as 'an unconsummated orgasm' (p. 159). It is described by Walsh (p. 232) as 'a waste of misdirected energy, misguided submission, and frustrated purpose'. The direction in which it was to move is indicated by Keats' addition of an induction; that beauty is right and should succeed seems, however, an inadequate philosophy.

Miltonic influence

Keats had been 'feasting upon' Milton in April 1818 and this influence shows. The poem is structurally based upon the first three books of *Paradise Lost* and the debate in hell in Book II is the source for Oceanus' speech. Unlike the Miltonic epic, however, the theme of 'Hyperion' is succession (i.e. transience) and the pathos of deposition (as in *King Lear*) rather than the more political act of dis-obedience and revolution which caused the expulsion of Satan from heaven. It uses the form of Miltonic **blank verse** and also his grand style, including adjectives after nouns, catalogues, and past participles. However, Keats was a fast-evolving and precocious poet who did not remain long in his Miltonic phase, soon moving on to a belief that 'English must be kept up'. He told Reynolds in a letter (21 September 1819): 'I have given up Hyperion — there were too many Miltonic inversions in it.'

The story

The poem's narrative is that of the deposition of the massive Titans, the earth's first gods, by Zeus/Jupiter, the leader of the Olympians, who become the new divine rulers of the world. This dramatic transfer of cosmic power had inspired many other poets, including Shelley in his *Prometheus Unbound*. Apollo, as god of poetry, represents the ascension of the new order to immortality whereas Hyperion, the old sun god, symbolised the tragic passing of the old order and cosmic mutability. But the moral and political theme is soon lost among the mystically religious and aesthetic emphasis Keats gives the poem, and its increasing subjectivity.

Book I opens *in medias res* with the melancholy scene of the deposed Saturn, chief of the Titans, sunk in grief and despair and being attended by a weeping Thea (Hyperion's wife), who fails to comfort the aged god. Hyperion appears and vows to resist the Olympians, but is persuaded to accept the inevitable with grace by the voice of heaven, Coelus, who preaches evolution rather than revolution, since the Olympians are more beautiful. In Book II there is a discussion between the fallen gods, who are becoming increasingly powerless and mortal, and therefore sensitive to pain, and Oceanus declares his faith in the natural process, i.e. change. Clymene says they should pin their hopes on the new god of song, Apollo, and ignore calls for war, which would be fruitless. Hyperion comes back. The brief and unfinished Book III describes the young god Apollo meeting with Mnemosyne, goddess of memory and a muse figure, who enables him to understand the immortal nature of poetry, and the godlike power of the artist.

'The Fall of Hyperion. A Dream'

Keats returned to the subject later the same year and tried to refashion 'Hyperion' into 'The Fall of Hyperion', but by late 1819 his failing health and other worries (money and Fanny) made it impossible for him to finish the second version either; and his friends let it be known that they preferred the first 'Hyperion'.

Similarities and differences

Keats' second attempt at epic ends as abruptly as the first, and is shorter. It is more tentative, exploratory and abstract; more subjective and concerned with the poet and poetry. There is less narrative confidence, or monolithic massiveness, though more by way of large cosmic themes. It has more actual dialogue and less apparent dialogue for rhetorical effect.

'The Fall of Hyperion' starts with an induction (lines 1–18), ending with a reference to Keats' own death. The adaptation of the first version starts at line 294 with the appearance of Saturn and Thea. It is less Miltonic than its predecessor, not only in making less use of Latinate phrasing, but also in being based on a medieval-style dream vision like Dante's *Divine Comedy*. Whereas 'Hyperion' deals with the transition of power, 'The Fall' is set after the event (the new title changes the emphasis from the character to his fate).

The story

The poem begins in **epigrammatic** style and develops into **allegory**; its similarities to Blake's work as a painter and engraver are the references to noise, movement, postures and other strong visual effects. It begins, in the persona's dream, in a mysterious forest and with the drinking of a heavenly juice which transports him to a temple where he struggles to climb the altar steps, having been warned that he will die if he cannot manage it. He meets Moneta, keeper of the sacred flame, with whom he has a dialogue on the correct attitude to poets and poetry, and devotes himself to the cause of true poetry. In return Moneta reveals herself as a vision of art, tragic and eternal, which corresponds to the fall of the Titans, and it is their shrine she is tending.

Mnemosyne/Moneta

Since the first version failed to unite idea and narrative, the second does not attempt to do so. Instead, Keats introduces Mnemosyne, mother of all the muses (usually but not always referred to as Moneta, whose name derives from the Latin for advice or warning), as a chorus and priestess who relates the defeat of the Titans. The poet introduces himself (to replace the Apollo figure from the first 'Hyperion') as her audience in order to explain to the reader the central idea. The link between the two

characters is the traditional one of the dream vision, which then makes Moneta's story a vision within a dream. The narrative is further complicated by another level of fantasy, as in 'La Belle Dame sans Merci', which takes the reader three steps from reality. Moneta is part of the vision and narrative of the gods as well as the figure outside of this who explains it, which is clumsy and confusing.

The objective viewpoint of the first version has been abandoned by Keats in favour of a subjective vision about himself and poetry. Moneta symbolises a perfection and harmony akin to that of 'Beauty is Truth', her face being a 'union of extreme suffering with great serenity' (D. G. James, quoted in Bate, p. 165). Keats was already concerned with tragedy in general and Shakespearean drama in particular, and fascinated by the connection between suffering and creativity. There is reason to believe that Keats had Cordelia in mind, with her patience and sorrow, who in *King Lear* is a bridge between the mortal and immortal, a Christian who 'dies into life' (III.130).

The message

The message of 'The Fall of Hyperion' seems to be: those who suffer too much die; those who suffer but attempt to comfort others, i.e. poets, can live. Memory leaves a trace and enables one to live on (which reminds us of Keats' need for fame and the fear of not achieving it revealed in his self-written epitaph: 'Here lies one whose name was writ in water'). That dreamers are ultimately useless is Keats' last word on the subject which preoccupied him throughout his poetic career. They inhabit an ethereal world without responsibility, whereas the poet remains in the garden of humanity and faces reality: 'The poet and the dreamer are distinct' (canto I.1.199).

Keats' letters

Keats' letters were first published in 1848. Most of them are personal, written to friends, family or fiancée. They have a playfulness, intimacy and directness and are full of sensitivity and detailed observation; they have an honesty, a self-awareness and an immediacy of language and thought which includes slang, bawdy puns, speculation, emotion, humour: content not considered suitable for inclusion in high poesy is expressed in a speaking voice through which a personality shines. A surprising number have survived, which suggests that the recipients considered them worth keeping. They contain a great deal of poignancy, especially for the reader who is aware of what would happen to Keats and suspects that he was aware too. Keats' last letter was written to Charles Brown from Rome on 30 November 1820, less than 3 months before his death and after he had given up writing poetry. The first letter we know of was a verse epistle 5 years earlier to a would-be poet.

The letters are an invaluable supplement to the poetry, commenting on variations and origins of particular poems. They explore the nature of poetry, the achievements of predecessors and contemporaries, and views on matters of poetic creation and aesthetic theory. Keats ranges over nearly every aspect of his life in a kind of stream of consciousness, sometimes referring to work in progress or including a draft. They also show outstanding wisdom, warmth and sincerity, giving an insight into Keats' experiences and his mind at work on a journey of self-discovery and on an evolution of poetic theory. They reflect the development of Keats' personal and creative life — the 'growth of a poet's mind', to steal Wordsworth's subtitle to *The Prelude*. T. S. Eliot believed that 'The Letters are certainly the most notable and the most important ever written by any English poet' and Wolfson (p. 121) states that there is a case for believing the letters to be the greater literary achievement.

The first major collected edition was that of H. E. Rollins in 1958, which consisted of 320 letters, some of which were to Keats (though he had a policy of burning old letters, which is a pity as his replies were interrelated). Reynolds, who replaced Hunt as Keats' mentor, was a major correspondent, receiving 9% of the total; 36% were to immediate family, particularly his brother George and sister-in-law Georgiana in America from 1819; 8% were to Fanny Brawne; the remainder were mostly to publishers and male friends.

Though it was common in the eighteenth and early-nineteenth centuries for nouns to be printed with initial capitals, Keats makes random use of capital letters, and there are occasional erratic spellings, although some, such as 'camelion', have changed since the early nineteenth century.

Extracts from the letters

...the passage in Lear — 'Do you not hear the Sea?' —has haunted me intensely...
(to John Reynolds, 17 April 1817)

...all the other beautiful Tales which have come down from the ancient times of that beautiful Greece.
(to Fanny Keats, 10 September 1817)

...a long Poem is a test of Invention which I take to be the Polar Star of Poetry, as Fancy is the Sails, and Imagination the Rudder.
(to Benjamin Bailey, 8 October 1817)

I am certain of nothing but of the holiness of the Heart's affections and the truth of Imagination — What the imagination seizes as Beauty must be truth...
(to Benjamin Bailey, 22 November 1817)

The Imagination may be compared to Adam's dream — he awoke and found it truth...
(ibid.)

O for a Life of Sensations rather than of Thoughts!
(ibid.)

'If I should die,' said I to myself, 'I have left no immortal work behind me [...] but I have lov'd the principle of beauty in all things, and if I had had time I would have made myself remember'd.' (ibid.)

...a man should have the fine point of his soul taken off to become fit for this world... (to John Reynolds, 22 November 1817)

...Negative Capability, that is when man is capable of being in uncertainties, Mysteries, doubts, without any irritable reaching after fact & reason... (to George and Thomas Keats, 21 December 1817)

...with a great poet the sense of Beauty overcomes every other consideration, or rather obliterates all consideration... (ibid.)

We hate poetry that has a palpable design upon us. (to John Reynolds, 3 February 1818)

I think Poetry should surprise by a fine excess... (to John Taylor, 27 February 1818)

...if Poetry comes not as naturally as the Leaves to a tree it had better not come at all... (ibid.)

I have great reason to be content, for thank God I can read and perhaps understand *Shakspeare* [sic] to his depths... (ibid.)

The world is full of Misery and Heartbreak, Pain, Sickness and Oppression. (to John Reynolds, 3 May 1818)

Axioms in philosophy are not axioms until they are proved upon our pulses. (ibid.)

I live in the eye... (to Thomas Keats, 27 June 1818)

When I am among Women I have evil thoughts... (to Benjamin Bailey, 18 July 1818)

Praise or blame has but a momentary effect on the man whose love of beauty in the abstract makes him a severe critic of his own Works. (to James Hessey, 8 October 1818)

I was never afraid of failure; for I would sooner fail than not be among the greatest. (ibid.)

The Genius of Poetry must work out its own salvation in a man: It cannot be matured by law and precept, but by sensation and watchfulness in itself. (ibid.)

I think I shall be among the English Poets after my death.

        (to George and Georgiana Keats, 14 October 1818)

I do not live in this world alone but in a thousand worlds.

        (to George and Georgiana Keats, 25 October 1818)

I feel assured I should write from the mere yearning and fondness I have for the Beautiful...   (to Richard Woodhouse, 27 October 1818)

I am ambitious of doing the world some good: if I should be spared that may be the work of maturer years — in the interval I will assay to reach to as high a summit in Poetry as the nerve bestowed upon me will suffer.   (ibid.)

...the poetical Character itself; ... that sort distinguished from the wordsworthian or egotistical sublime; ... it is not itself — it has no self — it is every thing and nothing — It has no character — it enjoys light and shade; it lives in gusto, be it foul or fair ... What shocks the virtuous philosopher delights the camelion Poet.

        (ibid.)

I have scarce a doubt of immortality of some nature or other...

        (to George and Georgiana Keats, 16 December 1818)

I am however young writing at random — straining at particles of light in the midst of a great darkness...   (to George and Georgiana Keats, 19 March 1819)

...the dream was one of the most delightful enjoyments I ever had in my life ... with a beautiful figure to whose lips mine were joined ... and in the midst of all this cold and darkness I was warm.

        (to George and Georgiana Keats, 16 April 1819)

Call the world if you Please 'the vale of Soul-making'.

        (to George and Georgiana Keats, 21 April 1819)

Do you not see how necessary a World of Pains and troubles is to school an Intelligence and make it a soul?   (ibid.)

I have two luxuries to brood over in my walks, your Loveliness and the hour of my death. O that I could have possession of them both in the same minute...

        (to Fanny Brawne, 25 July 1819)

I hate the world: it batters too much the wings of my self-will, and would I could take a sweet poison from your lips to send me out of it...   (ibid.)

I will imagine you Venus to-night and pray, pray, pray to your star like a Hethen [sic]   (ibid.)

I always somehow associate Chatterton with autumn...

(to John Reynolds, 21 September 1819)

I have given up Hyperion — there were too many Miltonic inversions in it...

(ibid.)

I am certain that I have said nothing in a spirit to displease any woman I would care to please: but still there is a tendency to class women in my books with roses and sweetmeats, — they never see themselves dominant.

(to Charles Brown, August 1820)

O, that something fortunate had ever happened to me or my brothers! — then I might hope, — but despair is forced upon me as a habit. ... I have coals of fire in my breast. It surprises me that the human heart is capable of containing and bearing so much misery. Was I born for this end?

(to Charles Brown, 1 November 1820)

Literary terms and concepts

Assessment Objective 1 requires 'insight appropriate to literary study, using appropriate terminology'. The terms below are relevant to the poetry of John Keats and will aid concise argument and precise expression.

allegory	extended metaphor which veils an underlying moral or political meaning
alliteration	repetition of consonants in adjacent words, especially initial letters, e.g. 'purple palace'
allusion	passing reference to another literary work, without naming it
ambiguity	capacity of words to have two simultaneous meanings in the same context, usually as a deliberate device for enriching the meaning of text
analogy	perception of similarity between two things
anaphora	the repetition of a word or phrase at the beginning of a series of poetic lines
anthropomorphism	attributing human characteristics to an inanimate object
antithesis	contrast of ideas expressed by balancing words or phrases of opposite meaning
aphorism	concise statement of principle based on experience
apostrophise	to address a divinity, object or abstract concept directly, e.g. Melancholy
archaic	diction or grammar no longer in current use at the time of writing, e.g. 'morn', 'yon', 'ye'

archetype	original model used as a recurring symbol, e.g. the femme fatale
assonance	repetition of vowel sound in adjacent words, e.g. 'sweet dreams'
Augustan	eighteenth-century, neo-classical, literary movement which imitated Roman writers who lived during the reign of Augustus (27 BC–14 AD)
ballad	narrative poem in short, rhymed verses, usually telling of love and travel
blank verse	unrhymed iambic pentameter, the form most used in Shakespeare's plays
caesura	deliberate break in a line of poetry, signified by punctuation
chiasmus	inverting the syntactical order of parallel phrases, e.g. 'No Asian poppy, nor elixir fine' (adjective–noun, noun–adjective)
classical	Greek and Latin prose or poetry style and content, typified by a restraint of feelings and form; particularly popular in the eighteenth century
cliché	predictable and overused expression or situation
compound	word made up from two others and hyphenated, e.g. 'fragrant- eyed'
connotation	association evoked by a word, e.g. 'rosy' suggests warm and healthy
consonance	repetition of consonants in adjacent words, e.g. 'slipper lips'
couplet	two consecutive lines of poetry which are paired in rhyme
diction	choice of words; vocabulary from a particular semantic field, e.g. religion
egotistical sublime	phrase of Wordsworth used by Keats, who deplored the former's tendency to focus excessively upon his own creative process
ekphrasis	description of figures as though they were art objects, e.g. Madeline in 'The Eve of St Agnes', the Titans in the 'Hyperion' poems
elegy	lament for the death or permanent loss of someone or something
elision	omission of letter(s) for metrical regularity in verse
end-stopped	pause created by punctuation at the end of a line of verse
enjamb(e)ment	run-on line of verse, usually to reflect its meaning
Enlightenment	philosophical movement of the eighteenth century which emphasised rationality, scientific thought and human rights; it led to the rise of democracy and contributed to the French and American revolutions

ephemerality	the concept that all things must pass; fleeting presence
epic	long, narrative poem telling a tale of heroic achievements over a period of time, often relating to national identity and with supernatural elements
epigraph	inscription at the head of a chapter, book or poem
epiphany	sudden and striking revelation of the essence of something sublime
epitaph	words engraved upon a tombstone
epithet	characteristic adjective
eponymous	main character after whom a work is named, e.g. Endymion
eternal verities	fundamental and permanent truths of human existence
eulogy	speech or writing in praise of someone or something
euphemism	tactful way of referring to something unpleasant or offensive
euphony	pleasant-sounding arrangements of words
fantasy	genre of fiction set in an imaginary world
foot/feet	division of syllables into a repeated metrical unit in a line of poetry
framing	a story within which another story is presented, as a parallel or contrast
genius loci	literally 'the spirit of the place', this refers to the Romantic belief that minor gods inhabit woods, streams and mountains
genre	type or form of writing with identifiable characteristics, e.g. epic
georgic	rural poem relating to agriculture, originating with Virgil's *Georgics* of 29 BC
Gothic	medieval genre, revived in the late eighteenth century, containing violence, death and horror; set in ancient buildings during darkness and bad weather
grand style	ornate, rhetorical, epic style derived from classical poetry
half-rhyme	words which almost rhyme, e.g. owl/soul
heroic couplets	lines of iambic pentameter rhymed in pairs; used in epic and mock epic verse
iambic pentameter	five feet of iambs, i.e. alternating unstressed/stressed syllables
iambic tetrameter	four feet of iambs
imagery	figurative descriptive language to build up atmosphere and convey themes in a literary work, usually in the form of simile or metaphor
in medias res	beginning a text in the middle of an event or dialogue

internal rhyme	placement of rhyming words within a line of poetry
interpolation	opinion which is inserted by the author into a narrative
invocation	summoning of a divinity or muse to aid the poet
irony	amusing or cruel reversal of an outcome intended, expected or deserved
juxtaposition	placing side by side for (ironic) contrast
legend	story about historical figure which exaggerates his/her qualities or feats
lyrical	expression of strong feelings, usually love; suggestive of music
memento mori	a reminder of mortality, such as a skull
metamorphosis	a fundamental transformation, such as from human to animal
metaphor	comparison implied, not stated, and not literally possible, e.g. 'my teeming brain'
metre	regular series of stressed and unstressed syllables in a line of poetry
myth	fiction involving supernatural beings which explains natural phenomena and embodies traditional and popular ideas
narrative	connected and usually chronological series of events which form a story
negative capability	Keats' desired state for a poet: 'capable of being in uncertainties, mysteries, doubts, without any irritable reaching after fact and reason'; the power to have no self
neologism	creation of a new word, usually in poetry, e.g. 'surgy'
octave/octet	eight-line unit of verse composing the first section of a Petrarchan sonnet
ode	lengthy lyrical and reflective poem addressed to the subject
onomatopoeia	words which imitate the sound being described, e.g. 'murmuring'
organic creation	belief of Romantic poets that artistic creation should arrive fully formed from the unconscious mind, like a plant from a seed
ottava rima	stanza of eight iambic lines containing three rhymes, invariably arranged as: ab, ab, ab, cc. First employed in fourteenth-century Italy by Boccaccio
oxymoron	two contradictory terms united in a single phrase, e.g. 'sweet pain'
pantheism	belief that divinity is manifested in aspects of nature
paradox	self-contradictory truth

pastoral	representing a simple, innocent and idyllic existence in the countryside; derived from classical writings
pathetic fallacy	attributing emotions to objects or natural elements to represent the persona's feelings
pathos	evocation of pity by a situation of suffering and helplessness
persona	created voice within a text who plays the role of narrator/speaker
personification	human embodiment of an abstraction or object, indicated by the use of capital letter or she/he
Petrarchan sonnet	eight lines (octave/octet) followed by six lines (sestet) with a turning point (strophe) between the two parts, rhymed abba, abba cdcdcd/cdecde
Platonism	belief of classical Athenian philosopher that this world is an imperfect reflection of the ideal which exists on a higher plane
plot	cause-and-effect sequence of events arising from characters' actions
poet laureate	national poet awarded the ancient honour of a laurel crown
portmanteau	joining parts of two existing words to form one new one, e.g. 'soother'
pre-Raphaelite	artistic movement of the mid-nineteenth century which sought to infuse art with moral qualities through the depiction of nature and worthy themes; considered art from Raphael (1483–1520) onwards to be morally degenerate
pun	word(s) with double meaning for humorous or enriching effect
quatrain	four-lined stanza or group of four lines of verse distinguished by their rhyme scheme
Renaissance	originating in Italy, the revival of the arts under the influence of classical models in the fifteenth and sixteenth centuries in Western Europe
rhetoric	art of persuasion using emotive language and stylistic devices
rhyme	repetition of vowel sounds in words at the end of separate lines of poetry
rhythm	pace and sound pattern of words, created by metre, vowel length, syntax and punctuation
romance	story of love and heroism, deriving from medieval court life and fairy tales

Romanticism	influential artistic movement of the late eighteenth and early nineteenth centuries, characterised by the rebellious assertion of the individual and a belief in the spiritual correspondence between man and nature
sensual	gratifying to the appetites of the flesh
sensuous	relating to the senses
sestet	verse of six lines; the last six lines of a Petrarchan sonnet
Shakespearean sonnet	three sections of four lines (quatrains) plus a final couplet, rhymed abab, cdcd, efef, gg
simile	comparison introduced by 'as' or 'like'; epic simile is a lengthy and detailed analogy
sonnet	lyrical poem of 14 lines of rhymed iambic pentameter, usually either Petrarchan or Shakespearean
Spenserian stanza	eight lines of iambic pentameter rhyming ab, abb, cbc, and a ninth line of iambic hexameter which rhymes with c; popularised in *The Faerie Queene*
stanza	another term for a verse; there are various forms depending on the number of lines and type of rhyme scheme
stereotype	category of person with typical characteristics, e.g. a knight
strophe	turning point within a poem
style	selection and organisation of language elements, related to genre or individual user of language
symbol	object, person or event which represents something more than itself, e.g. a rose
synaesthesia	evoking one kind of sensory experience with another; a blending of the senses, e.g. 'scarlet pain', 'perfume light', 'rosy eloquence'
synecdoche	substitution of the part for the whole, e.g. 'wings' for angel
syntax	arrangement of grammar and word order in sentence construction
theme	abstract idea or issue explored in a text
tone	emotional aspect of the voice of a text, e.g. 'miserable', 'ecstatic'
tragedy	literary work of a predominantly sorrowful nature, traditionally concerning kings or rulers; characterised by waste, a fall from power, and death

Questions & Answers

Essay questions, specimen plans and notes

The exemplar essay questions which follow can be used for planning practice and/or full essay writing within the time limit, with or without the text. Many have been previously set by different exam boards for various specifications. In each of the four sections there are essay titles with examiners' notes, further questions for practising, and some suggestions for ideas to include in a plan. Two questions are provided with sample student answers. Remember to talk about the poem and the persona, not the poet, and try to hear how the poem would sound if read aloud. The form and the language are essential elements of the poetry, so you must not restrict yourself to a discussion of content.

The question you choose may direct you to one or two prescribed poems or ask you to select your own. Either way you should think about the following:

- Careful selection of poems is crucial to ensure the relevance and success of your essay. The poems you like or are most familiar with are not necessarily the most appropriate for a particular title.
- Show your knowledge of the whole selection as well as your response to and analysis of particular poems.
- Focus closely on the chosen poem(s) but also relate their content and/or language to elsewhere in the selection; link your comments to the overall themes, and suggest ways in which the poem is typical of the poet's work as a whole.
- Do not waste time paraphrasing what happens in a poem; just give a quick summary of its setting and context, along the lines of who is present, where and why.
- Think about reader reaction, using your own as the basis for your response.
- In an open-book exam there will be annotations you have made in the margin and on the text, but only include the relevant ones, and remember that they need to be organised into a structured response, not just transferred to your essay as a list.

Poem-based questions: prescribed

1 **'Many of Keats' poems are meditative: he seems to use a poem as a way of putting into words and coming to terms with a state of mind.' Using a close examination of 'Dear Reynolds, as last night I lay in bed' as your starting point, consider this view of Keats' poetry.**

   AO1   The quotation itself offers candidates an explanation of 'meditative' and points them in a particular direction. Lower band candidates are likely to be selective in their approach to the quotation, possibly ignoring the internal 'definition' and focusing on 'meditative' without attempting to define it themselves, possibly focusing on 'state of mind' to the exclusion of everything else. Higher band candidates may well take 'putting into words' as a cue to consider poetry as process.

AO2i The final lines of the specified poem prompt candidates to consider genre and the inherent differences between poetry and prose. Reward against this AO will depend on the extent to which candidates pursue this and also on the type and range of other poems they choose to examine.

AO3 Candidates are likely to be divided here between those who focus on parts of the poem, looking perhaps at Keats' use of imagery in capturing states of mind, and those who also look at the poem as a whole, as a meditation 'putting into words...a state of mind' and coming to a conclusion. Breadth of analysis here will also be governed by a candidate's range of reference outside the specified poem.

AO4 Lower band candidates are likely to consider only part of the proposition and may do little more than talk loosely about mood in Keats' poetry, while higher band candidates are likely to consider the proposition in all its parts (and may even challenge it).

(Source: Edexcel mark scheme, June 2003)

2 **'Keats: the poet of the senses.' Explore your response to this view and the uses Keats makes of sensory perceptions by examining 'To Autumn' and any other appropriate poem (or section from a longer poem) of your choice.**

AO1 The key words that require understanding and defining are: *poet of the senses, view, uses, sensory perceptions, appropriate.* Higher band answers are likely to apply this understanding to the set task, addressing both text (the given poem and other appropriate poems) and task in an analytical and comprehensive manner, providing detailed supporting evidence for a range of arguments, while lower band answers are likely to show a basic awareness of these key terms, and rely more on description of the scene in the poem and Keats' main theme.

AO2i A key discriminator here is likely to be the range and choice of textual references within the candidates' answers. Higher band answers are likely to explore the generic features of the text (e.g. the ode form) and thoughtfully link this to the requirements of the task, while lower band answers are likely to be limited in their understanding of the text's generic features, the demands of the task and in the range of textual references made, frequently describing the poem's subject matter and main theme.

AO3 Higher band answers are likely to analyse Keats' use of language and structural devices (e.g. imagery and rhyme schemes) more closely than lower band answers, with a firmer grasp of the poet's intended effects. They are also more likely to see variety in the forms and language features adopted by Keats. Lower band answers are more likely to describe or narrate events or features of the text. How the candidates relate the given poem to their own chosen poem(s) are likely to be key discriminators.

AO4 Higher band answers are likely to explore a range of views and a range of textual supporting evidence in addressing, and possibly challenging, the task or main proposition in a direct and sustained way, while lower band answers are likely to accept the task or proposition and to describe and possibly exemplify the main theme, producing assertions, not arguments.

(Source: Edexcel mark scheme, June 2003)

3 'In many of his poems Keats starts out from the familiar and everyday but quickly takes us off into different territory.' In the light of this comment explore Keats' poetic methods in 'Ode to a Nightingale'.

Possible ideas to include in a plan

- 'I do not live in this world alone but in a thousand worlds' (letter to George and Georgiana Keats, 25 October 1818)
- heard bird singing (on Hampstead Heath in London); real but not exactly everyday experience (cf. 'Ode on a Grecian Urn')
- trigger for poem is a sublime appeal to the senses, in this case hearing
- different mental territory but not physical: movement from celebration of life to death wish
- nightingale changes from real bird to mythological character and symbol of history, immortality and romance
- description of journey into dark woods represents flight of fancy of persona
- 'viewless wings of Poesy' is the gateway to 'heaven's bourne' (Wasserman)
- language becomes ecstatic and kinetic ('I will fly to thee')
- fusion between heavy persona and light bird
- the 'return' pivot on use of word 'forlorn' between last two stanzas; comes back to earth and everyday world with a bump
- persona back in real world but unable to tell whether the experience was a dream
- typical of Keats to investigate the ambiguities and borderlines between waking and sleeping states
- reveals Keats' longing for immortality through poetry and his desire to escape the pains and mutability of this world

Further questions

4 With reference to 'Hyperion' and one other poem of your choice, discuss the use Keats makes of classical/Greek mythology in his work.

5 'A thing of beauty is a joy forever.' Discuss this claim with reference to 'Endymion' and one of the odes.

6 Critics have commented that the main impact of Keats' poetry lies in his use of imagery. Using 'Ode on Melancholy' as your starting point, explore the ways in which Keats uses images to present thoughts and feelings.

7 'The Eve of St Agnes' is a better narrative poem than 'Lamia'. How far do you agree with this judgement?

8 In the odes the poet seems to take up the position of mediator. With reference to at least two odes, discuss this claim and explain what is being mediated.

9 '"The Eve of St Agnes" is built up as a series of deliberate contrasts.' By means of a close examination of three distinct passages, explore Keats' varied use of contrast in the poem in the light of this comment.

10 'Keats characteristically gives visual form to the idea that human life is soon over.' Do you agree? You should base your answer on 'Ode on a Grecian Urn' and a poem of your choice.

11 Keats said that 'Poetry should surprise by a fine excess.' Discuss this remark in relation to two of the odes.

12 How is Porphyro presented in 'The Eve of St Agnes' — as a romantic lover or as a scheming seducer taking advantage of a young girl's naivety? You should refer closely to the poem to support your discussion.

13 Ricks says that 'Keats' poetry can accommodate what are ordinarily incompatible impulses'. How far is this true of 'Lamia'?

Poem-based questions: selected

1 Keats held that 'a long poem is a test of Invention'. Basing your answer on a close examination of *two* or *three* extracts from *one* of the longer poems, consider the ways in which Keats plays with narrative technique to sustain the reader's interest.

AO1 Although the question seeks to clarify the terms of the quotation by referring to 'narrative technique' in the context of sustaining 'the reader's interest', what is likely to distinguish candidates is their interpretation of both 'Invention' and 'test': lower band candidates are likely not to consider why a long poem might be construed as a test and therefore to discuss 'Invention' in isolation, interpreting it very possibly as 'innovation', while higher band candidates will see the two as interdependent and related to the effect of the poem on the reader.

AO2i The question focuses on 'long poems', and candidates are likely to be divided between those who seek to distinguish between these and other kinds of poem, and those who do not. Choice both of poem and of extracts will be key here, with some candidates considering only a limited range of narrative techniques, while others look at a variety of both narrative and other techniques.

AO3 In asking candidates to examine 'the ways in which Keats plays with narrative techniques', the question directs candidates to a consideration of structure; lower band candidates are likely to do little more than give instances of different types of narrative technique, while higher band candidates will consider Keats' deliberate manipulation of not only structure but language to achieve particular effects.

AO4 Lower band candidates are likely not to pursue the suggestion that long poems pose particular problems in terms of sustaining the reader's interest, while higher band candidates will explore the variety of ways in which Keats 'plays with narrative techniques', possibly relating their comments on this back to his own statement

about long poems being 'a test of Invention', and perhaps even questioning whether 'Invention' is necessarily an appropriate term to use to describe what he actually does in the longer poems.

(Source: Edexcel mark scheme, January 2001)

2 **'For Keats, *how* he writes about a subject or an idea is often more important than the idea itself.' Consider your response to this view. In your answer you should examine *at least two* poems or sections from the longer poems.**

AO1 The key words and literary terms in the task that require understanding and defining, and which are likely to be key discriminators, are: *how, idea, more important, subject.* Higher band answers are likely to apply this literary understanding to the set task, addressing both text (chosen poems) and task in an analytical and comprehensive manner, providing detailed supporting evidence for a range of arguments, while lower band answers are likely to show a basic awareness of these key words and literary terms, and rely more on description of scene, action or theme.

AO2i A key discriminator here is likely to be the range and choice of textual references within the candidates' answers. Higher band answers are likely to explore the generic features of the poems and thoughtfully link this to the requirements of the task, while lower band answers are likely to be limited in their understanding of the poems' generic features, the demands of the task and in the range of textual references made, frequently describing events and the poet's ideas.

AO3 Higher band answers are likely to analyse the poet's use of language (be it grammatical, structural, poetical or rhetorical devices) more closely than lower band answers, with a firmer grasp of the poet's intended effects. They are also more likely than lower band answers to see variety in the manner of the presentation of description, action, tone and themes. Lower band answers are more likely to describe features of the text and the poet's use of language. Discussion and analysis of the chosen poems, together with how they relate to the candidate's argument, are probably discriminators.

AO4 Higher band answers are likely to explore a range of views and a range of textual supporting evidence in addressing, and possibly challenging, the proposition in a direct and sustained way, while lower band answers are likely to accept the proposition and to describe and possibly exemplify the main theme, producing assertions, not arguments.

(Source: Edexcel mark scheme, June 2003)

Further questions

3 **'There is a tension in Keats' poetry between the "immortal spirit…free/As the sky-searching lark" which he creates, and the deliberate and precise poetic form which he adopts.' Do you agree? You should base your answer on a detailed examination of *two or three* individual poems or sections from one or more of the longer poems.**

4 What is the evidence, from *three* poems you have studied, that Keats was a Romantic poet?

5 Compare and contrast two of Keats' odes.

6 With close reference to *two* poems of your choice, discuss Keats' qualities as a narrative poet.

7 Examine Keats' ability to create contrasting atmospheres in his poetry by analysing two poems.

8 'What leaf-fring'd legend haunts about thy shape/Of deities or mortals, or of both,/ In Tempe or the dales of Arcady?' Explore Keats' poetic treatment of the scenes he takes from mythology. You should base your answer on a detailed examination of *two or three* individual poems or sections from several longer poems.

9 'Although its subject matter is abstract, Keats' poetry relies on close observation and description of the physical world.' Say whether you agree, basing your answer on a detailed examination of *three* individual poems or sections from longer poems.

10 'Romanticism consists of the strange, the exotic and the grotesque.' Illustrate the truth of this statement by exploring the themes and techniques of Keats' poetry. Select two or three key passages.

Whole-text questions: open book

1 How can the following quotation from 'Endymion' IV, 646–48 be applied to Keats' work as a whole?

> There never liv'd a mortal man, who bent
> His appetite beyond his natural sphere,
> But starv'd and died.

Possible ideas to include in a plan:

- consistent preoccupation in poetry with borderline between mortal/immortal
- appetite key concept in Keats — linked to senses and desires
- frequent use of word 'sweet' and related food and taste words
- starvation a metaphorical concept in Keats — nourishment needed for imagination
- death a recurring event or reference throughout work — and Keats' life
- early poems like 'The Eve of St Agnes' and sonnets advocate indulgence in the senses as escape route from harsh reality to happiness
- by last poems, e.g. 'Lamia', those who pursue unnatural appetites cut themselves off or are punished
- in 'Endymion' the poet learns to be satisfied with an imperfect realisation of the ideal
- but 'Fancy' (published 1820 and therefore a late opinion on the subject) seems to condone letting fancy roam since pleasure and beauty cannot otherwise be found in the everyday domestic world
- quotation is typical of Keats' philosophy of irreconcilable opposites: senses deceive but also sustain, and reason is an impoverished diet, inadequate for a poet

- Keats' work as a whole shows that mortals cannot avoid death and starvation whether they indulge in appetite or not, therefore they might as well have pleasure as well as pain

Further questions:

2 'What they want is a sensation of some sort.' How successful is Keats in fulfilling the reader's need?

3 Keats wrote 'death is the great divorcer for ever'. Look at how death is explored in Keats' poems.

5 Keats has been accused of 'vulgar sentimentality, pretentious straining for effect, and a cloying prettification of nature'. Do you find him guilty or innocent of these charges?

6 'Keats' language is guilty of an over-ripe lusciousness which can be excessive.' Is this a fair comment on Keats' poetic style?

7 'Pain is an integral part of Keats's vision of the world' — J. C. Smith.
'A delight in the life of the senses' — Robert Gittings.
Is it possible to reconcile these comments? In your answer you should refer to two or three poems.

8 Critics have observed that Keats' poetry is full of 'unresolved contraries'. What are the ideas and elements which cannot be reconciled?

9 'Keats cannot refrain from chasing any descriptive butterfly that turns up, and the reader finds it genuinely hard to follow him in his ramblings.' Is this a fair comment?

10 How does Keats' portrayal of women in his poems reveal his attitude to them?

11 Much of Keats' poetry was condemned by contemporary critics. They called it 'childish', 'disgusting' and 'recklessly wasteful'. How far do you agree?

Whole-text questions: closed book

1 Discuss the importance of Keats' fascination with classical myths and explore the ways he presents them in his poetry.

AO1 Technically accurate; sophisticated style; fluent and telling use of apt and varied vocabulary; cogent, well-structured argument.

AO2ii Sound knowledge and understanding of the poems and their contents.

AO3 Mature skills of analysis and synthesis; secure conceptual grasp.

AO5ii Has a grasp of the classical myth context; shows a detailed knowledge of the poems used to illustrate; explores what is special in the ways Keats presents the poems.

(Source: AQA Examiner Report, top band criteria, January 2003)

2 'The definition of genius is that it acts unconsciously' (Hazlitt). Does the work of Keats suffer from a lack of conscious thought?'

Possible ideas to include in a plan

- poems expression of own theories of art, i.e. that it must be inspired and derive from pure imagination
- 'We hate poetry that has a palpable design upon us' (letter to John Reynolds, 3 February 1818)
- letters reveal conscious thought applied to writing process, however, and paraphrase poems
- conscious thought is demonstrated in experiments with genre, form and rhyme, e.g. 'Isabella'
- Keats rewrote 'Bright star!...'
- 'Ode to a Nightingale' moves from sensual appreciation to theorising
- thought sometimes interfered too much, as in 'Hyperion'
- fusion of conscious and unconscious in 'Ode on a Grecian Urn'
- 'To Autumn' seems to come 'as easily as the Leaves to a tree', and has no apparent moral
- art that deceives by seeming natural is the ultimate achievement

Further questions

3 To what extent does Keats convey in his poetry 'the agony and strife of human hearts'?

4 Keats' poems are a 'general romantic protest against a purely scientific view of the world'. Say whether or not you agree with this verdict.

5 Keats described himself as a 'camelion'. How is this evident in his work, and what effect does it create?

6 'Keats' vision of the world is essentially comforting.' Do you agree?

7 Discuss the use and significance of nature in Keats' poetry.

8 Keats has been described as 'the daintiest of poets'. What do you think this means, and do you agree?

9 'Keats is a sculptor whose marble becomes flesh.' How does Keats achieve this transformation?

10 What evidence is there in Keats' poetry of his fascination with myth?

11 What are the characteristics of Romanticism that are exhibited in Keats' poetry?

12 How does Keats reveal in his poetry a desperate desire to escape from the harsh reality of the times in which he lived?

13 'The Romantic poets believed that they had an insight into an unseen order beyond what they saw with their eyes.' What evidence of this belief do you find in Keats' poetry?

Sample essays

Below are two essays of different types, both falling within the top band. You can judge them against the Assessment Objectives for this text for your exam board and decide on the mark you think each deserves and why. You will be able to see ways in which each could be improved in terms of content, style and accuracy.

Sample essay 1: open book

How does Keats reveal in his poetry his obsession with illness and death?

It would be surprising if Keats' poetry did not show evidence of an obsession with illness and death, given his personal experience of both. He lost his father, mother and younger brother, and saw from close quarters the effects of 'the fever and the fret' of consumptive disease before he contracted it himself. As a trainee surgeon he saw illness and death in all its brutality, and to such a sensitive observer it must have imbued his vision with tragic tinges. The references in his poetry to specific body parts — particularly throats, mouths and foreheads — reveal his fixation with the human body generally, and with the symptoms of the killer disease tuberculosis, known as the Romantic affliction not only because poets contracted it because of their lifestyle, but because they were attracted to its pathos and the paradoxical beauty of its physical manifestations.

The paleness which was the main outward symptom of the illness formed one of the key colour images in Keats' work, and some of his characters, like the ailing knight in 'La Belle Dame sans Merci', are described as 'fading' towards death in a similar way to that summarised in 'Ode to a Nightingale': 'Where youth grows pale, and spectre-thin, and dies.' Conversely, the dominant red imagery of the poems is associated with other symptoms: flushing, spitting blood, feverish cheeks and brows. Even the more cheerful poems, such as 'To Autumn', tend towards loss of warmth, diminution of colour, and absence: 'gathering swallows twitter in the skies'. Keats was ever conscious of the natural processes of flux, mutability and decline.

Because of a keen awareness of mortality — partly fostered by the recent death of the young poet Chatterton — Keats and his characters seek a means of attaining immortality through creativity, sublime happiness, and other escapes from the constraints of time and place and the sufferings of harsh reality. The immortals, including the nightingale, are envied; those who lose or give up their immortality and start to feel pain, like the Titans and Lamia, are pitied. Humans who have found bliss through union either die, like Lorenzo, are abandoned, like the knight, are transformed into phantoms, like Madeline, or abuse their love, like Lycius. Happiness is doomed.

'When I have fears...', actually written before his own tuberculosis was diagnosed, prophesies Keats' own death and reveals an early and justifiable preoccupation with the belief that he would die young. He also refers in his letters to impending death and wrote his own moving and ironic epitaph. There is no self-pity in the poems or the letters. He was, however, guilty of being 'half in love with easeful death' ('Ode to a Nightingale'), a death wish typical of the Romantics, who believed it was preferable to die early and 'with no pain', when still young and beautiful, rather than when old and blighted by ugliness.

Because Keats was consistently ambivalent about everything, and could not dissociate joy from pain, its opposite but composite, death is ever-present as the tragic threat to comic harmony in his poems, and in his letters he told Fanny: 'I have two luxuries to brood over in my walks, your Loveliness and the hour of my death. O that I could have possession of them both in the same minute.'

All one can do in the certain expectation of future illness and death — on Keats' recommendation and that of all of the Romantics — is in the meantime to live life to the full, observe every detail, indulge in every physical sensation, experience every emotion and turn every moment, even cloudy, melancholy ones, into a cause for ecstasy and cele-bration. Nature, art, beauty, truth, love and friendship are the only possible temporary antidotes to the 'World of Pains and troubles'. Therefore, the overall mood of the poetry, despite so many references to illness and death, is not one of morbidity but one of lusciousness, sweetness and delight.

Sample essay 2: closed book

How does Keats attempt to convey the 'Oneness of things' in his poetry?

Plato's theory of ideals, which influenced Keats' philosophy of life, embodied an appreciation of the oneness of all existence; and oneness of man with nature was a goal of Romanticism. The poet was considered to be in the best position to perceive and interpret the qualities of both and bring the two together through close observation and poetic expression. Though the Romantics believed in the primacy of the personal, the individual and the subjective, they used their own perceptions and desires to represent those of humanity as a whole.

Keats in particular may have felt driven to seek union and unity, a feeling of acceptance and belonging, given the number of separations and rejections he suffered in his private life. As a 'camelion' poet, Keats strove to reconcile and harmonise disparate elements of existence and experience. He explained in a letter: 'I do not live in this world alone but in a thousand worlds.' His aesthetic theory, as conveyed in his poems and letters, is a quasi-religious one of fusion through imagination and love. A poet who is also a qualified apothecary and would-be surgeon cannot help but be interested in the connections between the diverse elements of physical and emotional chemistry (linked, for example, by the phenomenon of blushing).

One of the techniques Keats employs to create fusion is that of the observer who empathises with the observed and shares his or her sensations and emotions. He advocated 'negative capability' as a means to lose the self in the embrace of the other. This is apparent in both the narratives and the odes, where the persona is even able to imagine the thoughts and feelings of a non-human creature or object, like the nightingale and

autumn. He was not particular about gender distinctions (it is unclear whether Autumn is male or female) and attributes similar characteristics and experiences to both – e.g. the knight is a passive victim of love in 'La Belle Dame sans Merci', whereas Madeline plays this role in 'The Eve of St Agnes'. Other attempted fusions are those between art and nature, reflection and sensation, love and death, all depicted by the two antithetical sides of the one Grecian urn. In other poems there is a move from the universal to the particular, or vice versa, embracing both, as in 'Bright star!...' where an analogy is made between the persona and a star, and between the beloved and the earth.

Time as well as place is conflated in his poems, so that no distinction is made between the classical, the medieval and the contemporary in the odes or the narratives; they are all linked by their settings, their subjects, and their reference to historical process, itself an acknowledgement of the Oneness of human experience repeated through the ages. The use of the supernatural, dreams and metamorphosis allows characters and events to evade the normal constraints of reality, so that mortals and immortals can meet and mingle in the same world, and 'heaven's bourne' (Wasserman) can be crossed by humans and the delights of paradise briefly enjoyed, as in 'Grecian Urn' and 'Lamia'.

Transformations – whether of bodies, seasons, or moods – are a process of blending two into one, and of blurring the distinctions and borderline between them: Lamia is both snake and woman; Autumn is tinged with approaching Winter; the 'melancholy fit' 'dwells with Beauty'. The eternal flux and flow of the world – which Keats admitted in a letter made him 'dizzy' – is his main preoccupation and the fundamental idea behind all his poetry.

Keats is famous for his use of sense imagery, and in particular for his insistence on the sense of taste, the one which brings together all of the others and is the most intimate. A recurrent Keatsian device is that of synaesthesia, whereby two or more senses are combined in a single image, as in 'rosy eloquence'. Stylistically, an effect of oneness is attempted through various choices of diction and device, such as compounds, puns, portmanteaux, and oxymorons, which all rely on doubling up. These usages exemplify his pleasure/pain principle, whereby joy is ever 'Bidding adieu' and about to be replaced by sorrow. This is human application of the fundamental and universal fact of ephemerality and mutability: nothing can last, and everything has its opposite, therefore one must come to terms with both extremes of sensation in order to feel that the 'sweet pain' of life is being fully experienced and appreciated.

The attempt is not in doubt, but the question remains whether Keats truly succeeds in achieving an effect of oneness, given disagreements between readers and between critics about his ability to reconcile opposites and resolve ambiguity. The main contradiction is whether the dreamer is inspired or deluded, and therefore whether fantasy is to be rewarded or punished. Since life is full of paradoxes, and Keats was in search of truth as well as beauty, he was perhaps doomed to fail in his quest for synthesis.

References and further study

Books

Abrams, M. H. (1953) *The Mirror and the Lamp: Romantic Theory and the Critical Tradition*, Oxford University Press.

Bate, W. J. (ed.) (1964) *Keats: A Collection of Critical Essays*, Twentieth Century Views series, Prentice-Hall.

Bowra, C. M. (1961) *The Romantic Imagination*, Oxford University Press.

Brett, R. L. (1969) *Fancy and Imagination*, Critical Idiom series, Methuen.

Brooks, C. (1942) *The Well Wrought Urn*, Harvest.

Coleridge, S. T. (1975) *Biographia Literaria*, Everyman.

Furst, L. R. (1971) *Romanticism*, Critical Idiom series, Methuen.

Gittings, R. (1968) *John Keats*, Heinemann.

Hayter, A. (1968) *Opium and the Romantic Imagination*, Faber.

Hough, G. (1953) *The Romantic Poets*, Hutchinson.

Hugo, H. E. (1957) *The Portable Romantic Reader*, Viking.

Matthews, G. M. (1971) *Keats: The Critical Heritage*, Routledge.

Motion, A. (1997) *Keats*, Faber.

Praz, M. (1951) *The Romantic Agony*, Oxford University Press.

Ricks, C. (1974) *Keats and Embarrassment*, Oxford University Press.

Watts, C. (1985) *A Preface to Keats*, Longman.

Wolfson, S. J. (ed.) (2001) T*he Cambridge Companion to Keats*, Cambridge University Press.

Essays and articles

Adams, R. 'Ode on a Grecian Urn: the final lines', *English Review*, Vol. 5, No. 1.

Bellairs, J. 'Variation on a vase', **www.bellairsia.com/articles/1965-variationsvase.html**.

Martin, T. 'Transformations and ambiguities in Keats' "Lamia"', *English Review*, Vol. 13, No. 3.

Newman, C. 'Exploring Keats' narrative poems', *English Review*, Vol. 13, No. 1.

Sutcliffe, J. 'Keats' composure', *English Review*, Vol. 10, No. 4.

Trilling, L. (1955) 'The poet as hero: Keats in his letters', in *The Opposing Self: Nine Essays in Criticism*, Viking.

Walsh, W. (1957) 'John Keats', in B. Ford (ed.) *The Pelican Guide to English Literature*, Vol. 5, Penguin.

The following articles are published on the University of Montreal's *Romanticism on the Net* website; access details are in the next section.

- Mizukoshi, Ayumi (Teikyo Heisei University): 'The cockney politics of gender – the cases of Hunt and Keats', *Romanticism on the Net*, 14.

- Sandy, Mark (Durham University): 'Dream lovers and tragic romance: negative Fictions in Keats's *Lamia, The Eve of St Agnes, and Isabella*', *Romanticism on the Net*, 20.

Internet

A good place to start is **www.john-keats.com**. This site contains the texts of all of Keats' poems: click on 'Poems' in the left-hand margin to go to a full list of titles. One advantage of internet texts is that they can be searched for words or phrases. For example, click on 'The Eve of St Agnes' and search for 'cold'; it appears three times in the poem. Alternatively, use the search function on the 'Poems' page to search for words or phrases in all of Keats' poems.

Another fascinating site is maintained by the Keats-Shelley House in the Piazza di Spagna in Rome (**www.keats-shelley-house.org**). Keats lived in the house during the last few months of his life. Following the link 'Keats' takes you to a biography, with special attention to the time he spent in the house, including illustrations.

Another major site is at **www.englishhistory.net/keats.html**. This comprehensive site includes texts of articles by contemporary critics of Keats' poems. These help to explain the initially hostile reception to his work. The site includes some highly informative articles and an excellent set of illustrations (which can be downloaded to illustrate a piece of work) including facsimiles of some manuscripts of Keats' poems.

All of these sites include extensive links to related sites. One link will lead you to a past British Library exhibition on Keats which contains a number of gems. The index page is at **www.bl.uk/whatson/exhibitions/keats.html**, and it includes facsimiles of the manuscript of 'Hyperion' and one of his letters, and a transcription to compare with the original. There is even a sound-recording of a nightingale which can be listened to while reading the 'Ode to a Nightingale'.

Another useful resource is the *Romanticism on the Net* website, **www.ron.umontreal.ca**, which contains both a list of all the articles and a search engine which operates in French.

For the study of the odes, there is an invaluable web concordance by the University of Dundee at **www.dundee.ac.uk/english/wics/keats/framconc.htm** which allows you to search for every use of any word in the odes of 1819. Finally, **www.thingsmagazine.net/text/t6/Grecian2.htm** has an important article on 'Ode on a Grecian Urn', by Rosemary Hill.